FAMILY MATH
The Middle School Years

Algebraic Reasoning and Number Sense

Virginia Thompson and
Karen Mayfield-Ingram

Principal Artist - Ann Humphrey Williams
Production Manager - Louise Lang

About EQUALS and FAMILY MATH

Since 1977, EQUALS has developed innovative mathematics curriculum materials to increase access and equity for all students and to help children everywhere realize success in mathematics. We have a special focus on traditionally underrepresented groups—females, students of color, and those from low-income and language-minority families. EQUALS, FAMILY MATH, and its Spanish counterpart MATEMATICA PARA LA FAMILIA serve PreK–12 educators, parents, and children. As leaders and experts in the fields of mathematics, equity, and bilingual education, our academic staff present workshops as well as write books for both home and classroom use.

For information about EQUALS and FAMILY MATH, additional book copies, or to receive our publications brochure, contact:

FAMILY MATH
Lawrence Hall of Science # 5200
University of California
Berkeley, CA 94720-5200

(510) 642-1823 - program
(800) 897-5036 or (510) 642-1910 - books
(510) 643-5757 - FAX
Web site: http://equals.lhs.berkeley.edu
Email: equals@uclink4.berkeley.edu

Credits:

Production Manager: Louise Lang

Cover and Principal Artist: Ann Humphrey Williams

Design: Carol Bevilacqua

Senior Editor: Carl Babcock

Editors: José Franco, Louise Lang

Photographer: Elizabeth Crews

Printing (last digit): 10, 9, 8, 7, 6, 5, 4, 3, 2

Table of Contents

Table of Contents

Number Sense

Tools for Parent Advocacy

More Resources

Acknowledgments

We wish to thank many sources for their support.

Funding for the initial development and dissemination of the FAMILY MATH program was provided by The Fund for the Improvement of Postsecondary Education of the U.S. Department of Education. The National Science Foundation and U.S. Department of Education funded further dissemination of the program to Spanish-speaking and English-speaking families. The Carnegie Corporation of New York provided funding for the publication and distribution of the *FAMILY MATH* book. This support allowed the creation of the program and its extensive dissemination throughout the United States and abroad.

The Charles A. Dana Foundation of New York provided funding for the development of activities that focus on the middle school curriculum and for the piloting of these materials.

The FAMILY MATH program has been called the daughter of the EQUALS program, which has promoted access and equity in mathematics education since 1977. Three retired staff members contributed significantly to FAMILY MATH: Nancy Kreinberg, the founding director of EQUALS, followed her vision to pursue and obtain significant funding for FAMILY MATH; Jean Stenmark supplied early activity ideas and went on to co-author both *FAMILY MATH* and *FAMILY MATH for Young Children;* Kay Gilliland brought many activities to the program, taught pilot family classes, and continues to lead FAMILY MATH inservices throughout the United States and abroad. We are especially indebted to these three colleagues. Their spirit and energy contributed significantly to the program. In addition, Ruth Cossey, co-author of *FAMILY MATH,* served as an inspiration for our work, especially at the middle school level.

We also want to thank our FAMILY MATH friends from around the world for their ongoing support. They are the parent, community, and teacher leaders of FAMILY MATH classes, the FAMILY MATH site coordinators and their staff, and our colleagues in the fields of mathematics, family involvement, educational research, and mathematics education.

We received suggestions and ideas from many individuals, including Eleanor Linn, Beverly Braxton, Rhett Rattley-Lewis, Len Cooper, and the late Robert Wirtz. We also want to thank Jorge López, Steve Jordan, and Daniel Orey for their recommendations and encouragement about mathematics content.

Teachers and staff of the California Renaissance Project attended our first middle school FAMILY MATH inservice workshops and piloted the first set of materials. We thank them for their dedication, time, and feedback.

This book is a collection of materials that works well in home settings, family classes, and the classroom. Many of the activities are variations of ideas that have appeared in various mathematics education publications. Some were brought to us by FAMILY MATH colleagues and are included with some modifications. These sources are acknowledged. Some of the activities are considered classics.

The following publications and projects were rich resources for ideas and would be of value for others who want more activities: The National Council of Mathematics (NCTM) journals: *The Mathematics Teacher, Mathematics Teaching in the Middle School, Teaching Children Mathematics;* the NCTM *Standards;* the NCTM *Addenda Series Grades 5–8;* the California Mathematics Council (CMC) *Communicator; Algebra* by Anita Wah and Henri Picciotto; and *Mathematics: An Informal Approach* by Albert Bennett, Jr. and Leonard Nelson.

The EQUALS staff members patiently supported us, providing ideas, insights, and encouragement, throughout the process of the development of this book. They are José Franco, director of EQUALS, Kathryn Baston, Terri Belcher, Bob Capune, Grace Dávila Coates, Carol Gray, Ellen Humm, Louise Lang, Gen Llamas, Angélica López, Deborah Martínez, Hilda Pérez-Espinoza, and Helen Raymond.

Most of all, we thank the families of FAMILY MATH—all of the adults and children—who have taken the program into their hearts and homes to make it what it is today.

Virginia Thompson
Karen Mayfield-Ingram
Lawrence Hall of Science
University of California at Berkeley

Introduction

In grades five through eight, families are asked to make many choices about which mathematics courses their children will take. These decisions will determine the math and science courses a child can take in high school. In turn, the high school courses a child takes affect future options for college majors and vocational and technical schools. Consequently, these middle school choices influence a child's career. All too often families receive little or no input about the long-term impact of these decisions.

In order to boost career options, it is vital for every student to take math and science courses throughout the middle and high school years. Certain groups—African Americans, Latinos, Native Americans, students from low socio-economic levels, and females—have often been denied access and the support necessary to succeed in advanced mathematics courses. While there has been some growth in achievement for these students, their representation in careers that require mathematics and science backgrounds continues to be a concern. Enrollment and success in advanced math and science courses open a path to future options for every student.

Surviving Adolescence

All parents want to support their children throughout their education. (Throughout the book, the term parents refers to all caregivers.) However, during the middle school years this can be challenging. Many parents and children feel as if they are constantly trying to catch up with each other. Simple communication often seems to be a challenge.

Middle school children are struggling with issues of control, autonomy, and identity. Self-confidence may become self-doubt. For example, girls who were very successful in mathematics at the elementary level often lose their confidence and underestimate their abilities as they enter their teens. In an effort to cope with these issues, many children build walls around themselves. It's natural for parents to feel rejected and back away. Just as children required help in making decisions and setting limits when they were younger, adolescents need guidance and support as they become more responsible for themselves.

Honey, I bought us a Parent Survival Kit to use until he goes to college.

Parents and children need new mechanisms to talk about what's going on in their lives. We hope the FAMILY MATH Middle School program will assist you in understanding today's middle school mathematics and its importance for your child's future. Our goal is for this book to help your family relate in a way that is educational and enjoyable for all.

FAMILY MATH—The Middle School Years

This book is the third in a series of FAMILY MATH books. All the activities are based on the National Council of Teachers of Mathematics *Standards for Curriculum and Instruction,* which outlines the appropriate type and method of instruction for students at various grade levels. Most of the activities involve several integrated math concepts rather than isolated skills. These connections promote better student understanding and mathematics achievement.

Our focus is algebraic reasoning and number sense. All students have studied arithmetic, and many have been introduced to algebraic thinking in the elementary grades. However, during middle school, children enter a new cognitive developmental stage that enables them to think more abstractly.

Algebra allows us to make insights or generalizations beyond what can be done at a concrete level. It is required for more formal work in practically all mathematics courses and many other disciplines—such as economics, psychology, sociology, biology, and engineering. Number sense allows us to see relationships between numbers, do arithmetic quicker, and know if our answers are reasonable.

Using lessons learned from our K–6 FAMILY MATH program, we included elements in *FAMILY MATH—The Middle School Years* that proved effective for all families, and are particularly critical for middle school. Using tools such as beans, blocks, toothpicks, diagrams, and calculators, families work cooperatively to analyze and solve problems. The aim is for parents and their adolescent children, regardless of their prior math experience, to engage and be successful in meaningful mathematics.

To adjust to the more advanced level of mathematics, we added a new type of activity. These activities require an investigative approach in which family members analyze, record, and draw conclusions about mathematical situations. They probe deeper into the concepts of middle school mathematics and promote the type of critical thinking children need for success in the 21st century.

Another new component in this book is the parent advocacy chapter. It provides a framework for families to make informed decisions about their children's math future. There are suggestions to assist parents in helping their child at home with homework—even if they aren't familiar with the math content.

A section on how to establish and lead a Middle School FAMILY MATH class series is also included. A FAMILY MATH class is an opportunity for both parents and children to talk about mathematics with others, and to discuss middle school life in general. The program goals are for families to learn more mathematics, and for parents to support and advocate for their child's mathematics education.

Beginning of Activity

Icon description below.

Sample Activity Page

Information in boxes, italics, or sidebars tells more about the mathematics involved in the activity or provides connections to other topics or future schooling and work.

Special sidebar may be here too...

sample illustration

Activity Types

The following icons indicate different types of activities. Some activities fit in more than one catagory.

 Openers: activities that work well as an opening station or whose first steps can be used as opening activities.

 Games: activities in a game format.

 Guided: activities that require leader direction.

MATERIALS

A list of materials
for this activity.

WHAT'S THE MATH?

This lists the math topics that
are involved in this activity.

How

• Gives background and directions for doing the activity.

• Each step is marked with a • .

• There is space in the margins to write notes about any special
adaptations your family has made for the activity. The book is meant
to be used, so feel free to write in it.

• There are some game boards that you may want to duplicate so you
won't have to tear out those pages. Game boards and markers can be
glued onto cardboard for durability or copied onto heavy paper.

Extension

• These notes provide
suggestions for
extending and varying
the activity.

Equity for all students requires a full range of opportunities that can stimulate each person to fully tap his or her interests and capabilities.

Equity for all requires challenge for all.

Everybody Counts, **p. 29.**

Algebraic reasoning

Introduction

Algebra—the word often evokes a strong reaction from people. For many adults and students, algebra is the cause of anxiety, confusion, and feelings of insecurity and self-doubt. There are people who had successful algebra experiences. However, many of them will admit they didn't really understand algebra's connection to the real world—particularly in those wonderfully puzzling train problems seen in most text books.

A passenger train leaves a depot 1.5 hrs. after a freight train has left the same depot. The passenger train travels 18 mph faster than the freight train. Find the speed of each train if the passenger train overtakes the freight train in 2.5 hrs.

The "gatekeeper" role algebra plays in a student's high school and college mathematics education, and the subsequent career implications, are causes for concern from both parents and educators. Without "successfully" completing a basic algebra course, it is difficult, if not impossible, to take the mathematics and science courses necessary for entrance into most four year colleges. Although algebra can be taken later at a community college, doing so forces students to play catch up.

During the middle school years, students may be sorted or tracked into as many as four levels of mathematics classes. Each class has its own content and instructional format. Usually only one of these levels leads to college preparatory courses in high school. Due to the wide discrepancy of resources within the educational system, socio-economically disadvantaged students and students of color are at risk.

Some school districts tackle the gatekeeper role of algebra by making algebra a requirement for high school graduation. Unfortunately, many students who enroll in mandatory algebra courses receive D or F grades. In order for all students to have access to the curriculum and succeed in algebra, new student support services, curriculum, teacher staff development, and more parental involvement are necessary.

Many mathematics educators—as well as people outside the field—have strong and differing opinions about how, when, and which children should learn algebra. Some are concerned that all students are not ready for algebra in the eighth grade and recommend that only the "top" students be allowed to take the course; the other students must wait until the ninth grade. Other educators feel that if pre-algebra concepts are developed from kindergarten through seventh grade, then all students will be ready for algebra in the eighth grade. Another group feels that all students should take a pre-algebra course in the seventh grade and then go into algebra the next year.

Needless to say, a consensus about when and how algebra should be taught does not exist. Parents are left on their own to decide what is best for their child. While we cannot tell you what is best for your child, we believe that many of the components of algebra are ideas that can be taught in earlier grades. Algebraic thinking can be developed from kindergarten on. Students can then take the formal course at the middle or high school level. We developed a list of questions—located in the *Tools for Parent Advocacy* section—to assist your family in making decisions about middle school algebra.

For a general overview of algebra, see *Algebra: What's It All About?* at the end of this chapter.

Before we begin, let's look at a list of the *"Big Ideas of Algebra"* (see next page). These concepts are key to the development of algebraic thinking and to the understanding and formal use of algebra. Watch for them in the activities you do in this chapter.

Now it's time to get started. REMEMBER, no formal algebra is necessary for the materials in this chapter. The activities are designed to develop and reinforce algebraic thinking. There are many ways to approach the different activities and puzzles. No one way is the only way. We include *Algebra Notes* for a few of the activities that illustrate the connection to more formal algebraic notation and concepts.

The Big ideas of Algebra

• Representation and Multiple Representation
You can represent an unknown as a letter and represent relationships between unknown quantities in equations and algebraic expressions. For example, you might let n stand for the number of books your sister has for school; if you have twice as many books, then the number of books you have is 2n. In addition, there are different ways to express or represent the same relationship, for example, x + x + x = 3x.

• Patterns
Some patterns can be recorded in algebraic symbols. For example, the pattern add two to whatever number you start with can be expressed by the equation y = x + 2.

• Proportionality
You can use equal ratios (proportions) to solve problems and make comparisons. For example, if pencils cost 96¢ a dozen, you can set up the ratio, $\frac{2}{12} = \frac{x}{96}$ to find the cost of two pencils.

• Variables
You can find the exact value of unknown quantities, called variables in algebra, by using appropriate algebraic techniques. For example, if you know that 5x = 15, dividing both sides of the equation by 5 tells you that x = 3.

• Functions
There are consistent relationships or rules, called functions, that connect two (or more) variables, so that any number from one group can be matched with only one in the other group. For example, if the relationship is y = 2x, then no matter what x you choose, you will be able to find a y that is twice x; that is, if x = 1, y = 2, and so on.

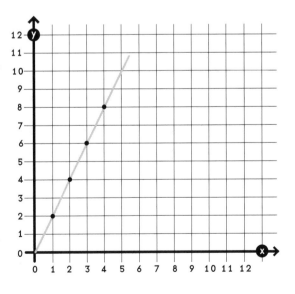

• Connection between Algebra and Geometry
Equations with two variables can be graphed on the Cartesian (two-dimensional) plane. For example, y = 2x is represented by the graph to the right.

• Applications
Algebraic techniques can be used to solve real-world problems. For example, you can use algebra to find the rectangular garden plot that will have the most area, when you have exactly 90 feet of fencing to keep the deer out of your community vegetable garden. ■

Buy One, Get one Free

The local poster store is having a Buy One, Get One Free sale on popular posters. When you buy a poster, you get the second one of the same or lesser value for free. Your task is to find out how to get the best deal.

Finding the best or optimum solution to practical problems is the basis of the branch of mathematics called *linear programming*. It is used in the field of *operations research*, which studies problems involving complex systems in business management, economic planning, and many other areas.

How

• The regular prices for the eight posters that interest you are:

Rock Star	$43
Movie Star	35
Sports Hero	40
Politician	11
Travel	8
Classic Movie	25
Old Advertisement	20
Nostalgia	13

• You decide you want one of each. You ask the clerk to pair the posters so that you get the next highest-priced poster free for each of the four posters you will pay for.

• As the clerk is working, his boss comes along and says that if you buy eight posters at once you will only get the four cheapest posters free! How does this affect your previous plan?

• Would it be worth coming in and buying only two posters at a time on each of four days? What difference would it make?

• A friend offers to help. She will choose four posters (two to pay for and the cheaper two for free) and you can choose four (two to pay for and two for free). Which four should each of you buy to save the most money?

Is there another plan that would save you more money? ■

Extension

• Bring information about a local sale. Discuss how to save the most money.

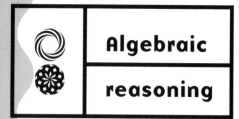
The Doubling Problem

There is a classic problem that appears in many middle school math books. It poses the question: Would you rather be paid $1,000 a day for 30 days or receive a penny on the first day, double that or 2 pennies on the second, and continue receiving double the previous day's pay for the 30 days? The growth of your income for the first of these types of pay is *linear* because you add the same amount each day. The growth for the second type of pay is *exponential* because your pay doubles or increases by a power of two each day.

The small raised number to the right of the 2 in 2^4 is called an *exponent* or *power*. It tells you how many times to multiply 2 by itself; so $2^4 = 2 \times 2 \times 2 \times 2$, or 16. When we write 2^4, we say *two raised to the fourth power* or *two to the fourth* for short. Raising a number to a power is an operation (like addition, subtraction, multiplication, and division) called *exponentiation*.

MATERIALS

paper

pencil

calculators

calendar

WHAT'S THE MATH?

Powers of 2;
comparison of linear
and exponential growth.

How

• Make a prediction as to which would be the best rate of pay.

• Work out with your family how much you will receive if you get $1,000 a day. Be ready to explain how you got your result to other families.

• Now you need to find out what happens in the doubling situation. You might want to construct a table or chart to help you compare the two types of pay. Calculators might also come in handy.

DAY	AMOUNT EARNED THAT DAY	TOTAL
1	.01	.01
2	.02	.03
3	.04	.07
⋮	⋮	⋮

• Which rate of pay is better?

Did it seem that way at first?

Are you surprised?

How would you explain what happens?

Extension

• Make a graph of the totals you would have after each work day.

Do the graphs help explain what happens?

How?

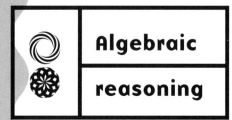

Algebraic reasoning

Half Empty, Half Full

The relationship of doubling is an example of an exponential function. The growth of exponential functions like 2^x is often surprising. These functions occur in applications of calculus. Bacterial populations in biology also grow this way. For example, cancer cells grow at an exponential rate.

The contents of the school pond are doubling every second.

At this rate it will take 10 seconds to fill the tank. How long will it take to fill half way?

How

• Work with your family and group to answer this question. Use diagrams or blocks to help you think about it.
Hint: If you get stuck, try *The Doubling Problem* first.

• Compare your results and approach with another group. ■

MATERIALS
pencil and paper
blocks or squares

WHAT'S THE MATH?
Exponential growth.

The Language of Algebra

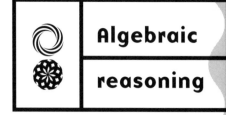
Mathematics has many linguistic features that present uncertainty for students, in particular for those whose primary language is not English. It is not enough to provide a formal definition of a term or to translate a math problem. It is critical to have time to talk about the mathematics. Help develop synonyms and other ways of looking at the problem in group discussions.

The ability to translate word phrases correctly into algebraic expressions is crucial not only in algebra, but in almost all higher mathematics and science courses. This skill is also indispensable on the job in fields such as economics, biology, geology, physics, and engineering.

Many algebra problems involve expressions like these: "three times as many," "24 more than," "5 more than three times as many," and "half as much." The *Blocks and Beans* and *Guess and Check* activities in this chapter give you ways to visualize and organize information to help you solve algebra problems. In order to do these activities, you will need to translate phrases from words into algebraic expressions correctly. One approach is to try the problem with fixed numbers, rather than an unknown. Look at what you tend to do automatically when you have a simple number like 10 or 20. Then apply the same method to the situation with an unknown.

MATERIALS

pencil

paper

calculators

WHAT'S THE MATH?
Algebraic language and expressions; proportional reasoning.

How

• Think about the expression "two times as much." What if someone said they were thinking of a number that is two times as much as 10? How would we find the number? — Multiply 2 times 10.

• Now someone tells you that today's secret number is two times as much as yesterday's number, which was called y. How could we write an algebraic expression that could help us find today's secret number if we knew yesterday's?

We know that today's number is twice as big as y, so the expression is 2y. In fact if we call today's secret number t for short, we could even write an equation: $t = 2y$.

The Language of Algebra

• Let's look at a more complicated expression: four less than three times as many.   First, how would we find a number that was four less than three times as many as 10 for example? We have to work backward and find out first what 3 x 10 is, then subtract 4. When we do that we have 30 – 4 or 26. Is 26 four less than three times ten?

• What if these numbers appeared in a story where we were told that Jennifer's age is 4 years less than 3 times Tim's age. How can we write an expression that tells us how to find Jennifer's age when we don't know Tim's?

Let's let t stand for Tim's age. Then we know that Jennifer's age (let's call it j) is 3t – 4. And so, we can write an equation: j = 3t – 4.

Working with Numbers

• Work with your family to write the expressions below using arithmetic.

1. Six more than 17.

2. Six less than 25.

3. Three times as large as 11.

4. Two less than three times as large as 11.

5. Three times the sum of 6 and 2.

6. One fourth of 20.

7. One fourth of 4 less than 28.

8. Ten less than the sum of 12 and 2.

9. Ten less than the result of 1,200 divided by 12.

10. Make up some new expressions to exchange with other family members and groups. Be sure to check the results before you exchange problems.

Using Algebra

• Write algebraic expressions for the following word phrases. If one seems particularly hard, try it with an easy number like 10 or 12 to help figure out what arithmetic is needed. Be ready to explain your work to other groups.

11. Tim's secret number is 24 more than Mary's.

12. Greg's secret number is 10 less than Helen's.

13. Your secret number is 6 times as large as mine.

14. Henry's secret number is ⅕ the size of Jean's.

15. Evan's number is 7 more than 4 times Jeff's.

16. Karen's number divided by 10 is 12 more than Judy's.

17. One fifth of Allen's number is twice as big as Joe's.

18. Make up some new expressions to exchange with other family members and groups. Be sure to check the results before you exchange problems. ■

TWICE AS MUCH . . . THREE MORE THAN . . . HALF OF . . .

Extensions

• Make up some expressions for your family and group to translate.

• Find examples of *algebraic language*, such as the phrases "three times as many," "twenty more than," and "half as much." Look for examples in newspapers and magazines or on radio or TV. Bring them to share in the next class.

The Guess and Check Method

What do you think of guessing in mathematics? Many people feel you have to know the one right way to solve a problem in order to get the right answer. However, educated guessing and estimating can often get you started when you are stuck and don't know where to begin. In fact, it may lead you to the answer you are looking for. In addition, a "guess and check" chart can often help you write the algebraic equation for the problem.

How

• Consider the following problem.

Sam collects hats and T-shirts. He has 4 more T-shirts than hats. Altogether he has a total of 20 T-shirts and hats. How many does he have of each?

• To get ready to do this problem by the guess and check method, we record what we know as headings in a "guess and check" chart. We'll start with shirts because that's what is mentioned first.

• We know Sam has 4 more T-shirts than hats. What do we do to figure out the number of hats he has? We need to subtract 4 from the number of T-shirts. So we note this information for the Hats column.

• What are some different possible numbers of T-shirts and hats for this problem? What if he has 25 T-shirts? How many hats would he have? What if he had 6 T-shirts? Or 50 T-shirts? Work with your family to find five more possibilities.

T-SHIRTS	HATS (T-Shirts — 4)
25	21
6	2
50	46

• Now focus on the whole problem. We know that Sam has a total of 20 hats and T-shirts, so we make a note of that when we put in a total column.

• We will make a guess for the number of T-shirts, say 10. That guess means he would have 10 – 4 or 6 hats. The total for these guesses is 16, but the problem says there are a total of 20 T-shirts and hats. This means we need to start guessing with a higher number.

MATERIALS

pencil

paper

calculators

WHAT'S THE MATH?

Solving algebra problems; ratios.

What about 16 T-shirts? That would give 16 – 4 or 12 hats, with a total of 28. Oops, that's too big. We need to go back to a smaller number. What about 14? That gives a total of 24, which is still too big. What about 12? Aha, that's just right!

T-SHIRTS	HATS (T-Shirts — 4)	TOTAL	COMMENTS (goal is total of 20)
10	6	16	too small
16	12	28	too big
14	10	24	too big
12	8	20	JUST RIGHT

• Let's set up one more problem.

A secret number is 8 more than a second number. Their sum is 72. What are the numbers?

• Let's start with a column for the secret number. How do we get the second number when we know the first? It is 8 less than the secret or first number. And the sum of the two numbers we are looking for is 72.

Now let's try some guesses for the secret number and see if we can solve the problem.

SECRET # (First #)	SECOND # (First # — 8)	SUM (goal is sum of 72)	COMMENTS
20	12	32	too small
30	22	52	too small
50	42	92	too big
40	32	72	JUST RIGHT

• Notice in these problems it doesn't matter which quantity you start to "guess" first, whereas in the *Block and Beans* activity you really need to start with the smallest quantity you are looking for.

The Guess and Check Method

• Work with your family and table group on the problems below. Start by setting up "guess and check" chart headings that reflect the information from the problem and then make educated guesses to solve the problem. Be sure to keep a comment column in your charts.

1. Two times a number is 2 less than 20. What is the number?

2. A hamburger costs $2.10 more than a large coke on special. Together they cost $3.30. How much does each cost?

3. A school pen costs 50¢ more than a school pencil. Together they cost $2.00. How much does each cost?

4. A shirt costs one third the cost of a pair of shoes. A jacket costs twice the cost of the shoes. Altogether these three items cost $220, how much does each cost?

5. Three times a number is 6 less than 30. What is the number?

6. The first number is 15 less than the second. Their product is 76. What are the numbers?

Algebra Notes

• The problems you have been working on are algebra problems. You have been solving for unknowns. The guess and check charts guide you through the arithmetic you need to do and provide a way to check your work. In addition, we can use their headings to set up algebraic equations for these problems. Let's look at some examples to see how this works. Look at the first problem, on page 12.

T-SHIRTS	HATS (T-Shirts — 4)	TOTAL	COMMENTS (goal is total of 20)

Let t represent or stand for the number of T-shirts. Then t – 4 will represent the number of hats. We also know that we want the total of T-shirts, t, and hats, t – 4, to be 20.

We can use this information to write an algebraic equation:
$$t + t - 4 = 20.$$

Adding the t's together, we have:
$$2t - 4 = 20.$$

Adding 4 to each side of the equation, we have:
$$2t - 4 + 4 = 20 + 4$$
or
$$2t = 24.$$

Dividing each side of the equation by 2, we have:
$$\frac{2t}{2} = \frac{24}{2}$$

So the number of T-shirts is
$$t = 12$$

and the number of hats
$$t - 4 = 8.$$

To check, we can add 12 + 8 to see that we do get 20.

• Look at the guess and check chart headings for the second problem, on page 13.

SECRET # (First #)	SECOND # (First # − 8)	SUM	COMMENTS (goal is sum of 72)

Let n represent the secret or first number. Then the second number is $n - 8$. We want their sum to be 72, so we can write the following equation:
$$n + n - 8 = 72.$$

Adding the n's, we have:
$$2n - 8 = 72.$$

Adding 8 to each side of the equation, we have:
$$2n - 8 + 8 = 72 + 8.$$

Dividing each side of the equation by 2, we have:
$$\frac{2n}{2} = \frac{80}{2}$$
or
$$n = 40.$$

This means that the secret number is $n = 40$ and the second number, $n - 8$, is 32.

To check, we add 40 + 32 to see that we get 72.

Algebraic reasoning

Algebraic Estimation

Understanding and using algebra is key to all high school and college math and science courses, and to all careers based in science and computer science as well as business administration, economics, and many trades. This activity provides an opportunity to focus on algebraic language. (You may want to do *The Language of Algebra* before you try this activity.)

MATERIALS

3-4 estimation jars

pencil and paper

paper bags for estimates

WHAT'S THE MATH?

Algebraic expressions and language; estimation; proportional reasoning.

Leader Notes

Prepare jars or containers to hold the items below, or other similar materials, in the proportions noted. Make up statements that reflect the numbers of each object in each jar. For example, if you have 20 jelly beans and 40 pretzels, you might write: there are twice as many pretzels as jelly beans.

Here are three examples of clues that might appear on your estimation jars.

Pretzels, Fish, and Marshmallows

Estimate how many pretzels are in the jar.
There are three times as many pretzels as fish crackers.
There are two times as many marshmallows as fish crackers.

Rainbow Shells, Rigatoni, and Rainbow Twists

Estimate how many of each type of pasta is in the jar.
The number of Rainbow Shells is 27 more than three times the number of Rigatoni.
The number of Rainbow Twists is twice that of the Rigatoni.

Licorice and Gum Drops

How many pieces of candy in all?
There are 43 more than 4 times as many licorice as gum drops.

How

• Work with your family. Use the proportions and other information to estimate how many of each item is in each jar. Discuss your strategies. Record your estimates on a slip of paper. Include the name of the jar and the initials for each member of your group. Place the papers in the appropriate estimate bags.

Hint: To get started, decide which object has the least amount and make a guess about the number of those objects.

• Your class leader will help you compare the estimates and let you know which ones are closest. ■

Extension

• Make up a new jar for next week. Be sure to include some information about items in the jar as hints to help others make their estimates.

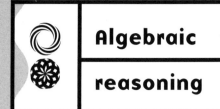
Four-Sock Drawers

Working with pairs of socks should add fun to this activity. You can find the answers to the puzzles by making lists and using a guess and check method, even though some of them could be solved by a more formal algebraic method. (You may want to do *The Language of Algebra* before you try this activity.)

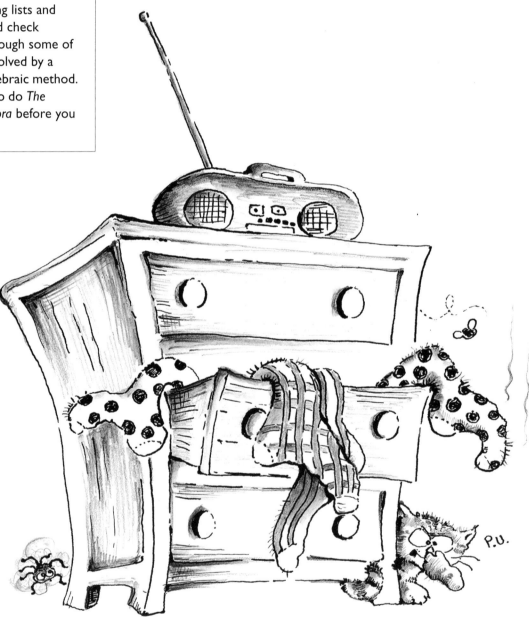

WHAT'S THE MATH?

Algebraic language; proportional reasoning; simultaneous equations; logical thinking.

How

• Each drawer contains black, red, blue, and white socks. Each sock is only a single color. Work with your family to find how many socks of each color there are in each drawer.

• You may want to try a combination of guess and check and algebra methods for Drawer 7.

• When you have solved the puzzles, make up sock drawer puzzles to share with others.

❊ Drawer 1 ❊
This drawer contains:
• Three times as many blue socks as black
• Two more blue socks than red
• One fourth as many black socks as white
• 20 socks in all

❊ Drawer 2 ❊
This drawer contains:
• Three blue socks
• A total of seven white or black socks
• In alphabetical order, one more of each color of sock than the color before

❊ Drawer 3 ❊
This drawer contains:
• Three more white than blue socks
• Twice as many red as blue socks
• Four more black than red socks
• A sock that could not possibly have a mate of the same color

❊ Drawer 4 ❊
This drawer contains:
• Twelve socks that are red or white
• Six socks that are black or blue
• Twice as many white as blue socks
• Half as many black as red socks
• One and a half pairs of blue socks

❊ Drawer 5 ❊
This drawer contains:
• 13 black socks
• Red and blue socks together that equal black socks alone (more blue than red socks)
• Less than half as many blue socks as white
• A list of sock numbers that is part of the *Fibonacci* series
• The *Fibonacci* series goes 1, 1, 2, 3, 5, 8, and so on

❊ Drawer 6 ❊
This drawer contains:
• Socks of all colors that do not have mates
• An equal number of blue and white socks
• 20 blue or black socks
• 22 black or red socks
• 16 red or white socks

❊ Drawer 7 ❊
This drawer contains:
• 482 socks
• 202 black or red socks
• 240 black or white socks
• 280 white or blue socks
• 242 red or white socks

❊ Drawer 8 ❊
• One more pair of black socks than red
• One more than twice as many white socks as black
• One more blue pairs than black pairs
• 12 red socks

Four-Sock Drawers

Algebra Notes

The guess and check method is very helpful in finding the solutions for the *Four-Sock Drawer* puzzles. Some of the puzzles can be easily solved using algebra alone. Look at the Drawer 2 puzzle.

Let b represent the number of blue socks, k represent the number of black socks, r represent the number of red socks, and w represent the number of white socks.

The first clue tells us that there are three blue socks. So b = 3.

The second clue tells us there is a total of seven white or black socks. Thus, we know that w + k = 7.

The last clue tells us that in alphabetical order, there is one more of each color sock than the color before. The alphabetical order of the colors is black, blue, red, white.

Therefore we know that
$$b = k + 1,$$
$$r = b + 1,$$
and
$$w = r + 1.$$

Since we also know that b = 3, we have 3 = k + 1.

Therefore, the number of black socks, k, is 2.

Since r = b + 1, we have r = 3 + 1 or 4 red socks.

And since w = r + 1, we have w = 4 + 1 or 5 white socks. ∎

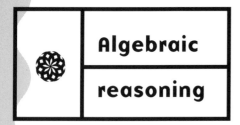

Algebraic reasoning

Blocks and Beans:
Visualizing Algebra Problems

Visualizing and modeling algebra problems and expressions with blocks and beans helps to build a solid foundation for translating word phrases into mathematics.

Have you heard the saying: "A picture is worth a thousand words?" For many adults algebra felt like a bunch of x's and y's that never made sense. Some of these people managed to memorize their way through the tests, while others just dropped out. For others the subject was so intimidating that they didn't even attempt it.

This activity provides a way to act out and visualize some beginning problems from algebra. It will help develop a foundation for more abstract ideas.

How

• Get some blocks or paper squares and beans, about 10 blocks and 20 beans for each person.

• Work with a partner. Have one person put out the blocks and beans and the other draw pictures to show what you did. We'll start with three traditional problems as examples.

Kevin has four times as many CDs as his younger sister, Benita. Altogether they have 25. How many CDs does each person have?

Benita's CDs

• First we need to figure out which person has the least number of CDs. Do you agree that it is Benita? Why? Put out one block (or square) to represent the number of CDs Benita has.

• How can we represent the number of CDs Kevin has? Since he has four times as many as Benita, we put out four blocks.

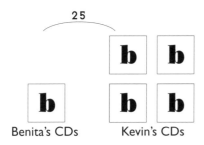

Benita's CDs   Kevin's CDs

• Now we have one block for Benita's CDs and four for Kevin's, with a total of five blocks. Remember, each block by itself stands for the number of Benita's CDs. Since there are 25 CDs altogether, that means each block represents 5 CDs. That would be 5 for Benita and 4 times 5 or 20 for Kevin.

*Karina has half as many school books as George. Together they have 9.
How many books does each one have to keep track of this semester?*

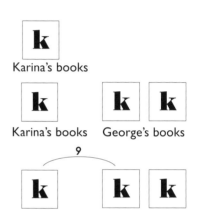

• First, who has the least number of books?   (Karina.)
Put out one block to represent the number of Karina's books.

• Now how many blocks do we need to represent George's books?
How many blocks do we need so Karina's blocks are half of George's?
(Two.)

• This means we have a total of three blocks that represent 9 books.
How much does each block represent? (Three.) So Karina has three
books to keep track of and George has six.

*Hilda is three years younger than Jaime. Together their ages add to 27.
How old is each?*

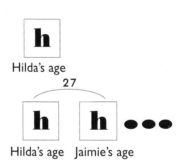

• Who is younger? (Hilda.) Put out one block to represent Hilda's age.

• If Hilda is three years younger than Jaime, that means Jaime is three
years older than Hilda. If we know Hilda's age, how do we find Jaime's
age? We need to add three. We will use beans. One bean for each of
the three years. Now we have one block for Hilda's age and one block
and three beans representing Jaime's age.

Altogether the numbers add to 27. Can you figure out how much each
block stands for?

• If we subtract three for the three beans, that leaves us with 2 blocks
representing 24 years. That's 12 years for each block, which means
Hilda is 12 years old and Jaime is 12 + 3 years old.

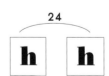

• Work with your partner and family members on the problems below.
Use blocks and beans. Be sure that at least one person keeps a record
in pictures of your work. Remember these problems usually work out
best when you start by asking what is the smallest number you are
looking for and letting one block stand for that number.

Blocks and Beans

1. A secret number is 8 times as big as another number. Their sum is 72. What are the numbers?

2. A school pen costs 40¢ more than a school pencil. Together they cost $3.00. How much does each cost?

3. A secret number is added to 6. That total is multiplied by 5 to get 50. What was the secret number?

4. Sam has 4 more shirts than pants. Altogether he has a total of 10 shirts and pants. How many of each does he have?

5. Jane is 7 years older than Jim. The sum of their ages is 35. How old is Jane?

6. There are three times as many cats on my block as dogs. There are a total of 16 dogs and cats. How many cats are there on my block?

7. One number is three times the other. Their sum is 88. How much is each number?

Extension

• Make up two problems to share with other families. Be sure to work them out before you exchange problems.

8. There is a family where each person weighs exactly twice as much as the next younger person. The total weight of the family, including the mother and father, was 504 pounds. The newborn baby weighs exactly 8 pounds. How many people are there in the family?

9. A cake is cut into 4 pieces so that each piece is twice as heavy as the preceding piece. The entire cake weighs 10 lbs. How much does each piece weigh?

The diagrams in this activity illustrate the formal algebra.
Let's look at the first and second problems.

First:
*Kevin has four times as many CDs as his younger sister, Benita.
Altogether they have 25. How many CDs does each person have?*

If we let b stand for the number of CDs Benita has and remember
that Kevin has 4 times as many CDs as Benita does or 4b CDs, the
diagrams help us to write an algebraic equation. We also know that
the total number of CDs is 25.

WORDS	DIAGRAM	ALGEBRAIC NOTATION
	[b] [b][b][b][b] = ⣿⣿	$b + 4b = 25$
Adding the b's we get	[b][b][b][b][b] = ⣿⣿	$5b = 25$
Dividing each side of the equation by 5, we get	[b] = ●●●●●	$b = 5$
Since Kevin has four times as many CDs, Kevin's CDs = 4b = 4 x 5 = 20		

For the next example:

*Hilda is three years younger than Jaime. Together their ages add to 27.
How old is each?*

If we let h stand for Hilda's age, the diagrams help us write the
following algebraic equations, using the fact that Jaime is three years
older than Hilda.

WORDS	DIAGRAM	ALGEBRAIC NOTATION
	[h] [h] ●●● = ⣿⣿	$h + h + 3 = 27$
Adding the h's we get	[h][h] ●●● = ⣿⣿	$2h + 3 = 27$
Subtracting 3 from each side of the equation we get	[h][h] = ⣿⣿	$2h + 3 - 3 = 27 - 3$
Dividing each side of the of the equation by 2, we get	[h] = ⣿	$h = 12$
Since Jaime is three years older than Hilda, we know that Jaime is 12 + 3 or 15 years old.		

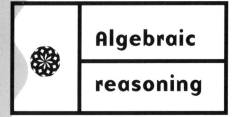
Math Behind the Trick I

Did you ever wonder how number tricks work? You can use objects such as paper squares and beans or buttons to figure out how some of these tricks work and learn some algebra concepts in the bargain. (You may want to try *Blocks and Beans* before you do this activity.)

HOLD ON! IT'S REALLY NOT THAT HARD ONCE YOU KNOW THE TRICK!

MATERIALS

paper squares and triangles or
square and triangular blocks

beans or other small markers

paper and pencils

calculators

WHAT'S THE MATH?
Algebraic language; variables;
using algebraic thinking to
analyze number tricks.

How

• First let's try a "secret" number in the example below.
Choose a number for your family to start with.

Example
Think of a secret number.
Add 5.
Multiply by 2.
Subtract 4.
Divide by 2.
Subtract your secret number.
Now you have 3.

• Did you get 3? Try some other numbers. Do you think you will
always get 3? Talk with your family about how you think this trick
works.

Analysis of the example with Squares and Beans
• Get about 10 small paper squares and 15-20 beans or other small
counters.

• Have one person write his or her secret number on the back of a
square so others can't see it. The square stands for or represents the
secret number. Have everyone put out 1 square and act out the
instructions for the trick. Ask one person to draw a sketch of the
squares and beans you have after each step.

• Add 5. Put in 5 beans to represent adding the number 5. Now we
have 1 square and 5 beans. *Note:* It doesn't say to add 5 of the
secret number, it just says to add 5. We can't use squares, we must
use beans.

• Multiply by 2. How can we do that with the square? Remember
that one way to think of multiplication is as repeated addition, so
when we multiply by 2 that's the same as adding two of the number.

For example 2 x 3 = 3 + 3; and 2 x 4 = 4 + 4.

Here we will have 1 square and 5 beans plus 1 square and 5 beans
or 2 squares and 10 beans.

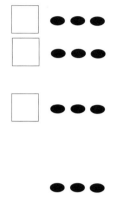

• Subtract 4.
Take 4 beans away. This leaves 2 squares and 6 beans.

• Divide by 2. The squares could make this harder. But we can think of dividing by 2 as removing one of two equal parts of what we have or removing ½ of what we have. There will be 1 square and 3 beans in each of the two groups or halves. So we have 1 square and 3 beans.

• Now subtract or take away the secret number. What's left? Three beans or 3.

• Did it matter what the secret number was? Discuss how using the squares and beans and acting out the directions for the trick help show what is going on and why you should always end up with 3 if everyone does the arithmetic correctly.

• Analyze the tricks below. Discuss why they work with your family. Are there any overall patterns you can find when you look at how they work?

Leader Notes

• In discussion, work to help participants see how using addition, subtraction, multiplication, and division makes these tricks work.

Working with a square to represent the secret number in a trick allows us to focus on the process of where the instructions lead us and how the trick works. The squares represent variables in algebra and are often written as x's or y's. A *variable* stands for a set of possible numbers that could satisfy a problem. You don't know which numbers work until you solve the problem.

This activity is interesting because it doesn't matter what numbers you start with, the result is always the same.

Trick A
Think of a number.
Double it.
Add 6.
Add your original number.
Divide by 3.
Add 5.
Subtract your original number.
(Now you have 7.)

Trick B
Think of a number.
Add 7.
Multiply by 2.
Subtract 4.
Divide by 2.
Subtract your original number.
(You have 5.)

Trick C

Pick a number.
Add 3.
Multiply by 2.
Subtract 4.
Divide by 2.
Subtract your original number.
(You have 1.)

Trick D

Pick a number.
Add 22.
Multiply by 5.
Subtract 25.
Divide by 5.
Subtract your original number.
(You have 17.)

Trick E

Pick two digits from 0 through 9.*
Think of them as a two digit number.
Start with the digit in the tens place.
Multiply the number in the tens place by 5.
Add 8 to this product.
Multiply by 2.
Add your original digit from the ones place.
(This is the first time you use this number.)
Subtract 16 and you will have the number you
   started with.

Hint: Use a square for the digit you put in the
   tens place and a triangle for digit you put in
   the ones place.

Extensions

• Work with a partner to make up a trick for a friend or family member.

• Try *Math Behind the Trick II.* In that activity, you will be able to tell people exactly what their secret number is.

• Look at the *Algebra Notes* for *Math Behind the Trick I and II.*

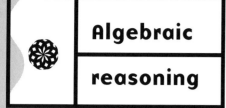
Math Behind the Trick II

In *Math Behind the Trick I,* all of the tricks end with a set number, no matter what people start with. The tricks in this activity end with different numbers depending on the starting secret number. However, you will be able work out each person's secret number. (You may want to try *Blocks and Beans* and *Math Behind the Trick I* before you do this activity.)

When you figure out the secret number, you are solving an algebraic equation. Algebra forms a basis for all future mathematics courses and is widely used in scientific and engineering fields as well as business and economics.

How

Example
Think of a secret number.
Add 7.
Multiply by 2.
Subtract 6.
Divide by 2.
Tell me what you have now and I will tell you your secret number.

Look at what you ended with and compare that number to your secret number. Discuss with your family how the trick works.

• To figure out the secret number, we will act out the problem with squares and beans as we did in *Math Behind the Trick I.* Have one person write a secret number on the back of a square so the others can't see it. Act out the trick with squares and beans in the middle of the table where everyone can see what happens. Ask one person to record the results of each step.

MATERIALS

paper squares and triangles

beans or other small markers

paper and pencils

calculators

WHAT'S THE MATH?

Algebraic language; variables; using algebraic thinking to analyze number tricks.

Analysis of the example with Squares and Beans

• Start by putting out 1 square to represent the secret number.

• Adding 7 gives 1 square and 7 beans.

• Multiplying by 2 is the same as adding 1 square and 7 beans to 1 square and 7 beans; so we have 2 squares and 14 beans.

• Subtracting 6 gives 2 squares and 8 beans.

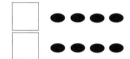

• Dividing by 2 is the same as taking half of what we have. There are two equal groups of 1 square and 4 beans each, so dividing by 2 gives 1 square and 4 beans.

• Now the instructions say, tell me what you have and I will tell you your secret number. How can we figure out the secret number when there is a total for the secret number plus 4? What can we do to get just the secret number? If we subtract 4 or take away 4 beans what is left?

• Try this trick several times as a group, starting with a different secret number each time. Can you figure out the secret number by subtracting 4 each time? Discuss how the squares and beans help you see how this trick works.

• Try acting out the rest of the tricks to figure out how to find the secret numbers. Discuss how they work with your family.

Extension

• With a partner make up a trick to share with a friend.

Math Behind the Trick II

Trick A
Think of a secret number.
Double it.
Add 9.
Add your secret number.
Divide by 3.
Add 3.
Tell me what you have and
 I will tell you your secret number.

Trick B
Think of a secret number.
Add 3.
Multiply by 2.
Add 4.
Divide by 2.
Tell me what you have and
I will tell you your secret number.

Trick C
Think of a secret number.
Add the next larger number*.
Add 7.
Divide by 2.
Tell me what you have and
I will tell you your secret number.

* *Hint:* to decide how to represent
this number using squares and
beans, think about how much
larger it is than the secret number.

Trick D
Think of a secret number.
Add 10.
Subtract 3.
Add 5.
Subtract 11.
Tell me what you have and
I will tell you your secret number.

Trick E
Think of a number.
Add the next larger number*.
Subtract 1.
Tell me what you have and
I will tell you your secret number.

Trick F
Think of a number.
Add the number* on either side of it.
Tell me what you have and
I will tell you your secret number.

Algebra Notes for Math Behind the Trick I and II

What kind of algebra is going on in these two activities?

Variables

When we use squares and triangles to represent secret numbers, we are using the concept of *variables*. Typically a variable is a letter or symbol used to stand for or represent an unknown quantity or number.

In algebra, you are more likely to see x's and y's representing unknown quantities, instead of squares or triangles.

Let's compare the example in *Math Behind the Trick I* using squares in one column and x's in the other.

To avoid confusion, we usually do **not** use x to stand for multiplication in algebra. For two times 3, we use a dot, 2•3. When a variable, such as x or y, is involved, you can just put it next to another variable or number and it means to multiply: 2x, xy.

WORDS	SQUARES & BEANS	ALGEBRAIC NOTATION
Think of a secret number	☐	x
Add 5	☐ •••••	X + 5
Multiply by 2	☐ ••••• ☐ •••••	$2 \cdot (x + 5)$ or $(x + 5) + (x + 5)$ $2x + 2 \cdot 5$ or $x + x + 5 + 5$ $2x + 10$
Subtract 4	☐ ••• ☐ •••	$2x + 10 - 4$ $2x + 6$
Divide by 2	☐ •••	$\dfrac{2x + 6}{2}$ or $\dfrac{2x}{2} + \dfrac{6}{2}$ $x + 3$
Subtract your original number		$x + 3 - x$
Now you have 3	•••	3

Algebra Notes for Math Behind the Trick I and II

Algebraic Language and Operations

When we use terms such as "multiply the secret number by 2" and "add the secret number to 6," and carry out these instructions, we are using algebraic language. We also performed arithmetic or algebraic operations using the variables (the squares and triangles).

Distributive Law

When we multiplied a result that had squares and beans in it, we used the *Distributive Law.* That mathematical law says we can either add the two parts or terms together and then multiply the sum, or multiply each of the parts by the number and then add. (We had to multiply first because we did not know the secret number.) This law also holds for division, to divide a sum of terms, we can add first and then divide or divide each term separately.

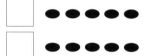

For example, in this trick, when we had to multiply one square plus 5 beans by 2, we got 2 times one square plus 2 times 5 beans or 2 squares and 10 beans. In algebra, we would have:

$$2(x+5) = 2x + 10.$$

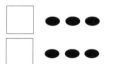

Similarly when we had to divide 2 squares plus 6 beans by 2, we got 2 squares divided by 2 plus 6 beans divided by 2 or 1 square plus 3 beans. In algebra, we would have:

$$\frac{(2x + 6)}{2} = \frac{2x}{2} + \frac{6}{2} = x + 3.$$

Solving Equations

For the puzzles in *Math Behind the Trick II,* we ended up with an equation to solve.

If your partner has 10 at the end of the instructions in the example in *Math Behind the Trick II,* the chart below shows the connection between the squares and beans and algebra. ■

WORDS	SQUARES & BEANS	ALGEBRAIC NOTATION
Your partner says, I have 10		$x + 4 = 10$
How do you figure out the secret number?		
In algebra a common way to record the thinking is the following		$x + 4 - 4 = 10 - 4$
or in words your partner's secret number is 6		$x = 6$

Cats and Canaries

Have you ever stared at a math problem and decided that there is no way you are ever, ever going to solve it. When you first work on the problems below, they could make you feel that way. But if you try a guess and check approach or draw a picture, you will find that they can be surprisingly easy. The title of this activity comes from the animals in the first problem. (You may want to try the *Guess and Check* and *Flowerpots* activities before this one.)

These problems can be written as a *system of two simultaneous equations.* There are many real-world applications for this type of system. For example, suppose you want to combine chocolate peanuts that cost 60¢ a pound with cashew nuts that cost $1.10 a pound, to make a mixture that cost $1.00 a pound. How many ounces of each do you put into each pound of mixture? What if the most you want to pay is 75¢ a pound?

MATERIALS
pencil and paper
calculators
activity cards

WHAT'S THE MATH?
Algebraic language; simultaneous equations; proportional reasoning.

How

• Have your group of 3 to 6 people select a puzzle. Pass out the clue cards. If there are extras, it's fine for some people to have two cards.

• You may read the information on your card aloud as many times as you wish. But you cannot give your card to someone else to read.

• Work together in your group to figure out the problem. Use any method or tools that you think will help, such as drawing diagrams, using blocks and beans, making guesses, or a combination of ways.

• When you have found a solution, check to see that it fits all of the clues.

• Compare your methods with other groups. Do you have a favorite?

• Try some other problems.

Extension

• Make up some problems for another group to try. Make sure you try them first to see that they work.

Cats & Canaries

- Ms. Lang keeps cats and canaries.

  She has 25 heads to pet.

  How many cats does she have?

Cats & Canaries

- Ms. Lang keeps cats and canaries.

  She counted three times as many cat paws as canary feet.

  How many cats does she have?

Cats & Canaries

- Ms. Lang keeps cats and canaries.

  The number of cat paws and the number of canary feet share common factors.

  How many cats does she have?

  (*Note:* A *factor* is a number which divides into another number evenly.)

Cats & Canaries

- Ms. Lang keeps cats and canaries.

  The total number of cat paws is a multiple of 5.

  How many cats does she have?

Cats & Canaries

- Ms. Lang keeps cats and canaries.

  The total of the number of cat paws and canary feet is divisible by 2, 4, 8, 10, 20, 40, and 80.

  How many cats does she have?

Cats & Canaries

- Ms. Lang keeps cats and canaries.

  The total number of canary feet is a multiple of 5.

  How many cats does she have?

The Ng Family

- There are 6 children in the Ng family.

  Each child has either a bicycle or a tricycle.

  How many bicycles does the family have?

The Ng Family

- There are 6 children in the Ng family.

  No child has both a bicycle and a tricycle.

  How many bicycles does the family have?

The Ng Family

- The oldest child says there are exactly 14 wheels altogether.

  How many bicycles does the family have?

The Ng Family

- Next year Dante will be old enough to ride a bicycle.

  Then there will be a total of 13 wheels.

  How many bicycles does the family have now?

The Ng Family

- Only the children have bicycles or tricycles in the Ng family.

  How many bicycles does the Ng family have?

The Ng Family

- The number of tricycles in the Ng family is a factor of the number of bicycles.

  How many bicycles does the family have?

Starfish and Octopi

Starfish & Octopi

- Mr. Ruiz keeps starfish (with five arms each) and octopi (with 8 arms each).

  How many starfish does Mr. Ruiz have?

Starfish & Octopi

- Mr. Ruiz has 24 mouths to feed.

  How many starfish does he have?

Starfish & Octopi

- Mr. Ruiz's son counted a total of 150 arms on the sea creatures.

  How many starfish does Mr. Ruiz have?

Starfish & Octopi

- The difference between the number of octopus arms and the number of starfish arms is 10.

  How many starfish does Mr. Ruiz have?

Starfish & Octopi

- The number of starfish arms is a multiple of the number of octopus mouths.

  How many starfish does Mr. Ruiz have?

Starfish & Octopi

- The difference between the number of starfish and octopi is less than 10.

  How many starfish does Mr. Ruiz have?

Farmer MacDonald

- Farmer MacDonald keeps cows and chickens.

  How many cows does she have?

Farmer MacDonald

- Altogether, Farmer MacDonald has 45 cows and chickens to feed.

  How many cows does she have?

Farmer MacDonald

- The vet told Farmer MacDonald that these creatures have a total of 110 feet.

  How many cows does she have?

Farmer MacDonald

- There are four times as many cow feet as there are cows.

  How many cows does Farmer MacDonald have?

Farmer MacDonald

- There is a difference of 30 between the number of chicken feet and the number of cow feet.

  How many cows does Farmer MacDonald have?

Farmer MacDonald

- The number of cows on Farmer MacDonald's farm is divisible by 2.

  How many cows does she have?

Cycles

Cycles

- Mary Ellen wants to make unicycles, bicycles, and tricycles with spare wheels and bike seats.

  How many of each can she make?

Cycles

- Mary Ellen has 26 seats to use to make unicycles, bicycles, and tricycles.

  How many of each can she make?

Cycles

- Mary Ellen has 60 wheels to use to make unicycles, bicycles, and tricycles.

  How many of each can she make?

Cycles

- Mary Ellen can make more bicycles than other types of cycles.

  How many of each type can she make?

Cycles

- The number of wheels Mary Ellen puts on bicycles is close to the number of wheels she puts on tricycles.

  How many of each type of cycle can she make?

Cycles

- Mary Ellen does not use very many wheels to make unicycles.

  How many of each type of cycle does she make?

Cats and Canaries

These problems can be written as two *simultaneous equations* with two unknowns. The goal is to find a solution that is true for both equations.

For example, in *Cats and Canaries,* if we let x stand for the number of cats and y for the number of canaries, we know the following. The total number of animals is 25, that is
$$x + y = 25.$$

We also know that the total number of legs is 80. Each cat has four legs and each canary has 2, so the number of cat legs is 4 times the number of cats, or 4x, and the number of canary legs is 2 times the number of canaries, or 2y, so
$$4x + 2y = 80.$$

Now we have two equations: $x + y = 25$ and $4x + 2y = 80$.

There are various approaches to solving these two equations for x and y. One idea is to find what x is in terms of y using just one of the equations, and then to substitute that result into the other equation.

Here we can look at
$$x + y = 25.$$

Subtracting y from both sides, we have
$$x + y - y = 25 - y;$$
thus
$$x = 25 - y.$$

Substituting this result for x in the other equation, that is, replacing x with 25 − y, we have
$$4(25 - y) + 2y = 80$$
$$4 \cdot 25 - 4y + 2y = 80;$$
thus
$$100 - 2y = 80.$$

Adding 2y to both sides, we have
$$100 - 2y + 2y = 80 + 2y;$$
thus
$$100 = 80 + 2y.$$

Subtracting 80 from both sides, we have

$$100 - 80 = 80 - 80 + 2y;$$

thus

$$20 = 2y.$$

Dividing by 2, we have

$$\frac{20}{2} = \frac{2y}{2} \; ;$$

thus $10 = y$, which is the same as $y = 10$.

Now we know the number of canaries is 10. Subtracting 10 from 25, that means there are 15 cats. To check, we need to see if

$4 \cdot 15$, the number of cat legs plus

$2 \cdot 10$, the number of canary legs is equal to 80.

Well,

$4 \cdot 15 = 60$ and $2 \cdot 10 = 20$
and their total is 80.

The answers check. ∎

Algebraic reasoning

Flowerpots I

This activity appears to be a set of simple guess and check procedures. However, it provides a background for finding numbers that satisfy two or more equations simultaneously.

Simultaneous equations with two unknowns can represent many real-world problems. For example, suppose there are two types of tickets being sold for the next school concert – box seats and bleachers. If you know the total number of tickets sold and the prices of the two types of tickets, you can work out the number of each type of ticket sold.

This activity is based on the work of Robert W. Wirtz.

MATERIALS

beans or counters

Flowerpots I puzzle cards

WHAT'S THE MATH?

Simultaneous equations
in two unknowns.

The garden center director loves flowers and mathematics. She has
a bunch of round and square flowerpots and has agreed to prepare
two flowerpots, one round and one square, for each resident in the
local retirement center. A group of students has volunteered to help.
The garden center director is delighted, but also wants to include
some mathematics in the project.

She decides to make a puzzle like the one below for each pair of
pots. The puzzle gives the total number of plants in the two pots
and the difference between the number of plants. The students must
figure out how many flowers to plant in each pot. Can you help
them?

How

• Use beans or counters to help you figure out how many plants go in
each pot. Move the beans around until the sum (total) and the
difference are correct. For each puzzle, there is only one answer for
the number of plants in the circular pot and one answer for the
number of plants in the square pot.

$$\bigcirc + \square = 7$$
$$\bigcirc - \square = 1$$

• What did you try first? What worked out in the end?
How did you get there?

• Work with your family to solve the other flowerpot puzzles.

Look for patterns that might help you with Puzzles 9 to 12.

$\mathbf{F}$lowerpots I

1. $\bigcirc + \square = 8$
   $\bigcirc - \square = 4$

2. $\bigcirc + \square = 10$
   $\bigcirc - \square = 4$

3. $\bigcirc + \square = 12$
   $\bigcirc - \square = 6$

4. $\bigcirc + \square = 11$
   $\bigcirc - \square = 5$

5. $\bigcirc + \square = 18$
   $\bigcirc - \square = 0$

6. $\bigcirc + \square = 17$
   $\bigcirc - \square = 1$

7. $\bigcirc + \square = 23$
   $\bigcirc - \square = 15$

8. $\bigcirc + \square = 30$
   $\bigcirc - \square = 6$

Extensions

• Work with your family to make up some problems for another family. How can you be sure that the numbers you choose for the sum and difference will work?

Are there any number combinations that won't work?

• Puzzles 9 to 12 take quite a few beans. Can you think of a way to solve them without having to use beans? What have you observed so far that might help you? Try your approach on these puzzles.

9. $\bigcirc + \square = 96$
   $\bigcirc - \square = 4$

10. $\bigcirc + \square = 100$
    $\bigcirc - \square = 76$

11. $\bigcirc + \square = 200$
    $\bigcirc - \square = 50$

12. $\bigcirc + \square = 80$
    $\bigcirc - \square = 48$

When you worked on the puzzles, you might have written a shorthand set of equations to represent the information on the garden center's cards. For example, for Puzzle 4:

$\bigcirc + \square = 11$ Circle + Square = 11
$\bigcirc - \square = 5$ Circle - Square = 5

If we replace the circle with an x and the square with a y, we have:

$$x + y = 11$$

and

$$x - y = 5,$$

which is called a *system of two simultaneous equations*. The goal is to find x and y so that both equations are true.

There are several approaches for solving such a system of equations. Consider what would happen if we added the two equations together.

We would have
$$x + y + x - y = 11 + 5.$$

Writing x + x as 2x, we have
$$2x + y - y = 16,$$

which is the same as
$$2x = 16$$

because y - y = 0.

Dividing by 2, we get
$$x = 8.$$

To find y, we can substitute our new found value of x, and we have
$$8 + y = 11.$$

Subtracting 8 from both sides gives
$$y = 11 - 8 = 3.$$

To check, substitute in the second equation using 8 for x and 3 for y:
$$8 - 3 = 5,$$
which is true.

Flowerpots I

Another interesting aspect of systems of two simultaneous equations is to explore how they relate to coordinate graphing. Take a grid sheet and number it for a graph as illustrated.

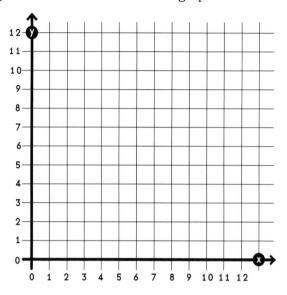

Now we will plot the graphs for each of the equations.

First look at x + y = 11 and make a table of numbers that make the equation true. Then do the same for x − y = 5.

Plot the first graph in one color and the second in a different color. You will have two straight lines. How many places do the two lines cross? What do you notice about the intersection point? What are its coordinates? How do they relate to the solution we found for these equations?

For x + y = 11

x	y
0	11
1	10
2	9
3	8
.	.
.	.
.	.
7	4
8	3
.	.
.	.
.	.

For x − y = 5

x	y
12	7
11	6
10	5
9	4
8	3
.	.
.	.
.	.

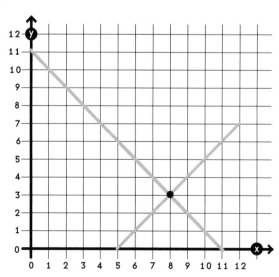

Try plotting the equations for some other puzzles. ■

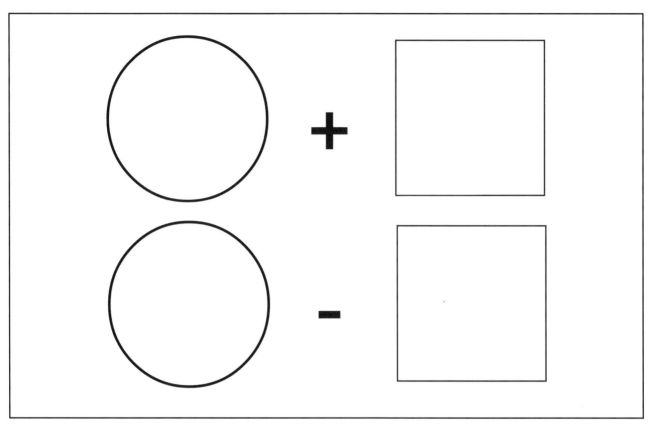

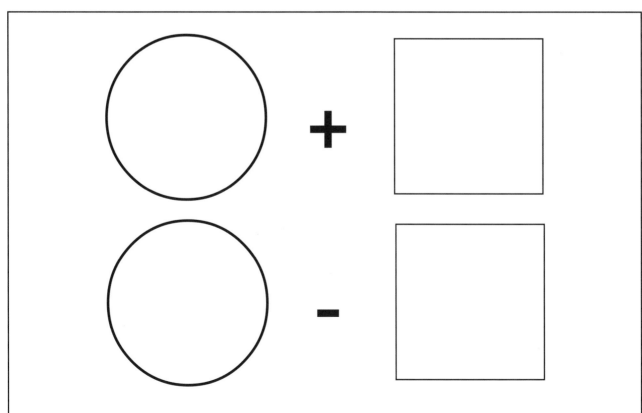

Flowerpots II

The guess and check method works well in this activity. The procedures are just a little more complicated than those required for *Flowerpots I*. However, here we are developing the algebraic foundation for solving three simultaneous equations or a *system of equations in three unknowns*.

Simultaneous equations can be used to solve real-world applications that have several conditions or constraints in fields such as physics, economics, and business.

This year the garden center director decides to give three differently shaped flowerpots full of flowers to each retirement center resident. She has round, square, and triangular-shaped flower pots.

Again, she decides to put some mathematics into the planting procedure. She prepares a puzzle for each set of three pots. The puzzle tells the total plants in each possible pair of the three pots. Can you help her figure out how many plants go in each pot?

How

• Use beans or counters to figure out how many plants go in each pot. Start with one of the totals and work from there. Move the beans around until all of the totals are correct. The numbers between pots indicate the total plants for those two pots.

Remember, for each puzzle, there is only one answer for the number of plants in the circular pot, one answer for the number of plants in the square pot, and one answer for the number of plants in the triangular pot.

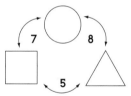

• How did this work out? Where did you start? How did you continue? Did you get 2 plants for the square pot, 5 for the circular pot, and 3 for the triangular pot?

• Try the next example. Discuss with your family the best place to start.

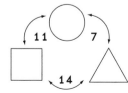

Where did you start this time? Did the task go faster? What did you get?

This activity is based on the work of Robert W. Wirtz.

WHAT'S THE MATH?

Simultaneous equations in three unknowns.

• Try the puzzles below.

1.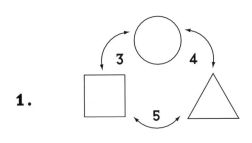

2.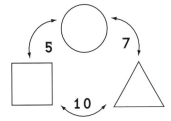

3.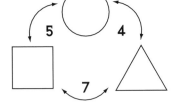

4.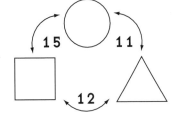

5.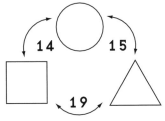

6.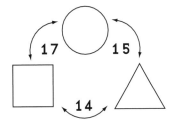

• Did everyone get the same solution for each puzzle? Is it possible to get more than one solution? What short cuts did you find to help you? Do you notice any patterns that occur for each of the cards?

Flowerpots II

Extensions

- Make up some puzzles for another family. Experiment with different numbers. Be sure to check that they work. Will just any group of three numbers work? Exchange puzzles with another group.

- Read the *Algebra Notes* to see what you have been doing in terms of algebra.

• Use what you learned on the problems below.

7. You have three squashes: one acorn, one summer, and one zucchini. Weighed two at a time, the weights are 5 pounds (summer and zucchini), 7 pounds (summer and acorn), and 8 pounds (acorn and zucchini). How much does each weigh?

8. I have one bale of hay, alfalfa, and barley. Weighed two at a time their weights are 90 kilograms (hay and barley), 70 kilograms (barley and alfalfa), and 40 kilograms (alfalfa and hay). How much does each bale weigh?

9. The computer made a big mess of the time reports. It said that Jennifer and Jose had worked a total of 50 hours, but not how much each had worked. Then it said that Marta and Jose had worked a total of 70 hours. And finally that Marta and Jennifer had worked a total of 60 hours. Can you help the students work out how much each should receive if they are paid $8 an hour?

Algebra Notes

When you worked on the puzzles, you might have written a shorthand set of equations to represent the information on the garden center's cards. For example, look at Puzzle 2.

Puzzle 2

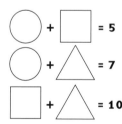

If we replace the circle with an x, the square with a y, and the triangle with a z, we have:

$$
\begin{aligned}
1. &\quad x + y = 5 \\
2. &\quad x + z = 7 \\
3. &\quad y + z = 10
\end{aligned}
$$

or a *system of three simultaneous equations in three unknowns*. The goal is to find x, y, and z, so that all three equations are true.

There are several approaches for solving this kind of system of equations. One way is to add or subtract two of the equations, find one of the unknowns in terms of the other two unknowns, and then substitute it in the other equation. This sounds complicated, but is not so bad when you do it slowly.

Subtract equation 2 from equation 3:

$$y + z - x - z = 10 - 7$$

or

$$y - x + z - z = 3.$$

Since z − z = 0, we have
$$y - x = 3.$$

Adding x to both sides, gives
$$y - x + x = 3 + x$$
or $$y = 3 + x.$$

Going back to equation 1 and substituting 3 + x for y, we have
$$x + 3 + x = 5$$
or $$2x + 3 = 5.$$

Subtracting 3 from both sides, gives
$$2x + 3 - 3 = 5 - 3$$
or $$2x = 2.$$

Dividing both sides by 2,
$$\frac{2x}{2} = \frac{2}{2}$$
or $$x = 1.$$

Now that we know that x = 1, we can substitute for x in equation 2 to find z:
$$1 + z = 7.$$

Subtracting 1 from both sides, gives
$$1 - 1 + z = 7 - 1$$
or $$z = 6.$$

Now, substitute 6 for z in equation 3:
$$y + 6 = 10.$$

Subtracting 6 from both sides, gives
$$y + 6 - 6 = 10 - 6$$
or $$y = 4.$$

So we have x = 1, y = 4, and z = 6.

The last thing to do is to check to make sure all of the equations are true with these numbers:

1. $1 + 4 = 5$
2. $1 + 6 = 7$
3. $4 + 6 = 10.$

Hooray!!!

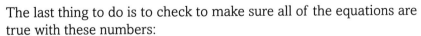

...to survive, students must have math skills through Algebra. While the expectation is not that a person will have the required "formula" memorized, it is expected that the person can adapt it to solve for the unknown. We are forever looking for the unknown and trying to back the answer. Students must be able to "figure" to put things in perspective.

**David Reeves,
Engineer, Chevron,
Personal Communication.**

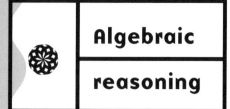

Getting to the Point

Plotting points on a two-dimensional graph or *Cartesian plane* allows us to represent algebraic expressions in a geometric or pictorial manner. It unites algebra and geometry, provides an insightful way to analyze problems from both areas of mathematics, as well as predict possible outcomes. Graphs are used in medicine, business, economics, and many other fields.

René Descartes is credited with creating the idea of using a two-dimensional coordinate system (now called the *Cartesian plane*) to represent algebraic equations.

WHAT'S THE MATH?

Cartesian coordinates; plotting equations; connecting algebra and geometry.

How

x	y=2x
4	8
2	4
6	12
.	.
.	.
.	.

Making a Table
• Make a T-table for number pairs that fit the following rule or pattern:

> *the second number is two times the first number.*

• Have everyone call the first number x and the second y. (This is a common convention for mathematicians. There is no particular reason to use x and y — some people might choose f for the first number and s for the second. But most mathematicians eventually settle on x and y.) Using x's and y's, we can write an equation that fits our rule: y = 2x, where 2x is an abbreviation for two times x.

• Compare the number pairs in your table with those of another family or group. Are some of the pairs different? Some the same? Are more pairs possible?

• Combine all of the data into one table.

Getting to the Points
• Now you are ready to plot the number pairs from your tables as points on a graph. Use the graph paper on page 247 or number your own graph the same way.

• Place markers such as buttons or beans on the numbers along the horizontal line, or *axis,* labeled x, to represent the first numbers in your table. (If you don't have all of these first numbers in your table, you can add them now, together with their matching second numbers.)

Getting to the Point

• Move each marker up vertically until it is across from the matching number in the y column of your table. For example, the marker on 1 moves up vertically until it is opposite 2; the marker on 2 moves up until it is opposite 4, and so on.

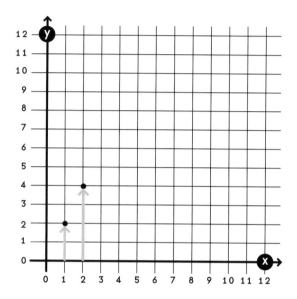

• Study the results. Do you see a pattern?

• Make a dot at the intersection under each marker. The point where the first marker was placed (moving up from 1 on the x axis opposite 2 on the y axis) is written as (1, 2) and read the point one, two. Check out the name of other points you have marked with your family. They are based on the first and second numbers in your table. The convention is to always say the horizontal axis number first.

• Are there other places on the grid that would fit the rule for your table? What about (0.5, 1.5) or (1.5, 3)?

• Do you think we could fill in enough number pairs to make a solid line?

Naming the Graph

• The answer to the last question is yes. The algebraic name mathematicians would give the line is $y = 2x$.

Plotting Other Rules

• Start by making a table, and then using markers on a graph; or go directly to the graph and apply the rule to each number on the x axis. When you find its y partner, you'll know how far up to move vertically.

• Try the following rules:

the second number is one more than the first ($y = x + 1$);

the second number is one less than the first ($y = x - 1$);

the second number is four more than the first ($y = x + 4$);

the second number is half of the first ($y = x/2$);

the second number is the same as the first ($y = x$).

Extensions

• Make up a rule of your own to try. (If you make up a rule that gives you a negative value for a y, they move down vertically until you are opposite the negative number.)

• Think about the following questions.

Will all rules result in graphs that are straight lines?

How can you tell?

What makes a graph steep or flat?

Is there a way to make a graph slant the other direction?

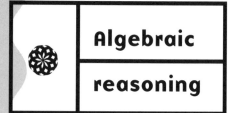
Hundreds Charts to Descartes I

"Skip counting" (counting by 2's, 3's and so on) on a hundreds chart results in interesting patterns on the charts themselves. These patterns can be converted to graphs on the *Cartesian plane*. (If you are unfamiliar with plotting points on a graph, you may want to try *Getting to the Point* before you do this activity.)

René Descartes was the first person to write about the idea of using a coordinate system to represent algebraic equations. A graph or "picture" of an algebraic equation can greatly simplify solving some problems. For example, instrument calibration and conversions, such as engine rpm to miles an hour, can be done using graphs.

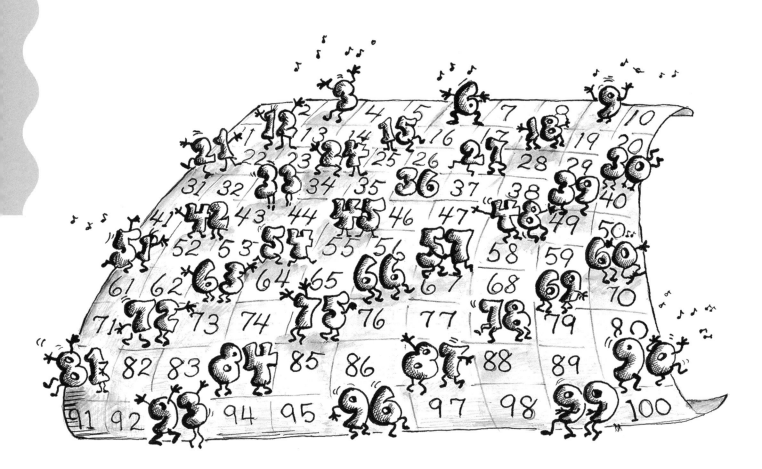

MATERIALS

hundreds charts (see page 252)

counters and colored pens

graph paper (page 247 or 248)

calculators

How

Creating and Recording Patterns

• Work with a partner or two other people.

• Use the addition constant feature on a calculator to skip count by 2's. (To do this on most basic calculators, you enter $2 + = = = ...$. Check the calculator direction pamphlet if this does not work. Ask your partner to place a marker on the hundreds chart for each number as you call them out. (If you don't have calculators, you can count by 2's directly on the hundreds chart.)

• Record your results in a table like the one to the right.

• Does anyone in your group have an idea for an equation or rule that tells how to find the value of the number you land on if you know the number of the marker? If the marker number is 4, what is the value? If it is 6, what is the value? What do you do to the marker number to get the value?

n: number of marker	V: value of number landed on
1st	2
2nd	4
3rd	6
4th	8
.	.
.	.
.	.

• Can you predict what the value will be for the 14th marker? For the 26th marker? How did you figure these out?

• What if you wanted a more general rule or equation for finding the value for any marker, for example the "nth" marker? How could you find the value of the number you would land on? How could you write what you did? You might say: the value is twice the marker number. But what would a mathematician do? They like to write equations, which are really abbreviations of the sentences we write in words.

If you think about any marker number, n, what do you do to n to get the value, v? Some people might give the equation $v = 2n$ right away, while others might need to test out more specific examples. It doesn't mater what letters you use for the unknown, as long as you are consistent.

Hundreds Charts to Descartes I

Making a Graph
• Now let's look at a way to make a pictorial representation of our table of the pattern of skip counting by 2's.

• Use graph paper like the one below with lines that are numbered along the horizontal and vertical axes or make your own.

Note: When negatives appear in front of the numbers, you move left on the horizontal axis and down on the vertical axis.

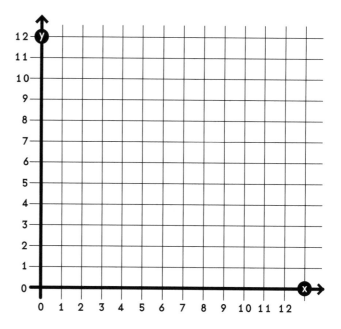

• Think of each entry in your table as an ordered pair: (1, 2), (2, 4), (3, 6), and so on. The first number tells us how far to move to the right from 0 along the horizontal axis. The second number tells us how far to move up from 0 on the vertical axis.

• Before you plot a point for each ordered pair in the table, make a prediction about what pattern the points will make. Then plot the points.

• What pattern are you getting? Do you think it's OK to connect the points to make a straight line? If you do that, it looks like the line would go through points like (0.5, 1) and (1.5, 3). Do they fit the pattern in the table?

If you extend the line, can you find other points that would fit from the line? Now you have a graph of $v = 2n$ (or $y = 2x$).

• If you were to count by 3's, 4's, or 5's, what do you think will happen? Will the graph be a straight line again or a curve? Will the graph be above or below the line that was generated when we counted by 2's? Explore these questions with your family. Plot the results for each graph in a different color.   Be ready to share your results.

Even though using n and v in our equations might help us remember what we were counting or looking at originally, mathematicians would commonly label these graphs as: $y = 3x$, $y = 4x$, and $y = 5x$, and so on, where x represents the number measured on the horizontal axis and y represents the number measured on the vertical axis.

• Here are some questions to think about: What will the graph for the equation $y = x$ look like? What rule or function will give us a graph or straight line below $y = x$ (closer to the horizontal axis)? ■

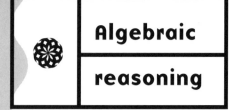

Hundreds Charts to Descartes II

Many patterns you make on a hundreds chart can be represented in a very different way as graphs on the Cartesian plane. Experiment with the patterns below and see what happens. (If you are unfamiliar with plotting points on a graph, you may want to try *Getting to the Point* before you do this activity.)

How

• Work with a partner.

• Get a hundreds chart and some markers. Cover the numbers whose digits add to 10. For example, 64 has the digits 6 and 4, which add to 10, as does 46. Describe the pattern of markers on the chart to your family members.

• Make a table to record your results.

x	y = 10 - x
0	10
3	7
5	5
4	.
.	.
.	.

Enter the first digit and the second digit for each pair that adds to 10. What are some of the number pairs in the table? Call the first column x and the second column y. You can write an equation for the rule for this table: x + y = 10.

Mathematicians have a convention of writing rules or functions in a form where you start with y =. Do you have any ideas for how to change x + y = 10 into this format? What if you subtract x from both sides of the equals sign or equation?

Then you have: x − x + y = 10 − x, or y = 10 − x, because x − x is 0.

WHAT'S THE MATH?

Coordinate graphing; converting patterns to equations and graphs.

• Talk with your family and partners and predict what you think will happen when you plot these number pairs as coordinate pairs on a graph. Plot them. Discuss your results.

• Pick another rule that involves digits on the hundreds charts and explore. Two suggestions are: the digits add to 12; and the difference of the digits is 2, when you take the smaller digit from the larger like 68 or 86.

• Make tables for each of your rules. Predict what will happen when you graph the new rules and how they will compare to $x + y = 10$. Be ready to share your results with others at your table. ■

Extension

• Some lines slant to the left and some to the right. What do you think determines the slant?

Patterns to Graphs

There are connections between geometric patterns, number patterns, and graphs on coordinate grids. In this activity, you will explore number patterns that geometric patterns generate, and see what happens when you plot patterns on a coordinate graph.

Recognizing patterns is extremely important in all branches of mathematics, not to mention in everyday life. Finding the algebraic relationship or rule, or *function*, that connects two sets of numbers is a very important skill that can be applied in all fields that use mathematics. For example, every lighthouse has its pattern of flashing lights for identification; many musical compositions are built from patterns of chords.

MATERIALS

toothpicks or small sticks

beans, buttons or other markers

graph paper (page 247 or 248)

WHAT'S THE MATH?
Connecting geometric patterns to algebraic rules and graphs.

How

Building Patterns
• Make a square using four toothpicks or sticks.

Add another square at the lower right corner. Add another square at the upper right corner of the last. Continue the pattern, adding one square each time. Make a table to record the pattern, the number of squares, and the number of toothpicks used at each step.

STEP #	PATTERN	# OF SQUARES	# OF TOOTHPICKS
1		1	4
2		2	8
3		3	12
4		4	16

Note: # means number

• Study the results in your table. If you continued until the 10th step, how many squares would there be in the pattern? How many toothpicks? What about the 20th step? How do you figure out the number of squares? The number of toothpicks? Can you explain how to do this to another group?

• What if someone wants to know how many squares and toothpicks for any number of steps? Can you describe what you get in general? Suppose you are at the nth step. How many squares would there be? (There would be n squares.)

What about the number of toothpicks? Did you discover the pattern for toothpicks is four times the number of squares? When we are at the nth step, the number of squares is n and the number of toothpicks is 4 x n or 4n. Or we can say that the rule for finding the number of toothpicks in this pattern is 4n.

Patterns to Graphs

Making a Graph

• Let's see how we can use the numbers from the pattern to make a graph. Look at the part of your table that lists the step number and the number of toothpicks. Write the numbers in pairs.

STEP # n	# OF SQUARES	# OF TOOTHPICKS	(n, t = 4n)
1	1	4	(1, 4)
2	2	8	(2, 8)
3	3	12	(3, 12)
4	4	16	. . . . . .

Note: The points you have plotted all fit the rule t = 4n, that is the number of toothpicks is equal to the number of the step, or term, x 4. Number pairs like (0.5, 2) and (1.5, 6), (0.4, 1.6) fit the more general rule: y = 4x; but because we are talking about only whole squares and whole toothpicks here, we can only plot the points that the step numbers, or terms, give us. The graph for this pattern will look like a series of dots on some of the intersections of the grid paper. When you plot the general rule, y = 4x, you can connect the dots to form a straight line.

• Plot the pairs on a coordinate graph. Do you see a pattern?

• What happens when you write number pairs for the step numbers and number of squares? What does this graph look like?

• Try Pattern A on the *Pattern Page*. Build it. Record your results and make pairs and plot the Step # and number of triangles. Then make pairs for the Step # and number of toothpicks and plot those points.

• Try the other patterns on the *Pattern Page*. What shapes of graphs do you have if you connect the points? Are they all straight lines?

• Can you create a pattern that does not result in a straight line? ■

Patterns to Graphs

	1st STEP	2nd STEP	3rd STEP	4th STEP	5th STEP
A					
B					
C					
D					
E					
F					
G					
H					
I					

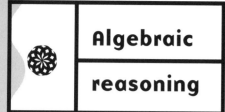

Graphs to Equations

It is possible to work "backwards" from a coordinate graph to create a table of points that are on the graph and use that to find an algebraic rule or equation for the graph.

Reading points from a graph is very important in algebra and other higher courses in mathematics. Recognizing and generalizing patterns is important in all of mathematics and its applications, such as predicting fashion trends and weather.

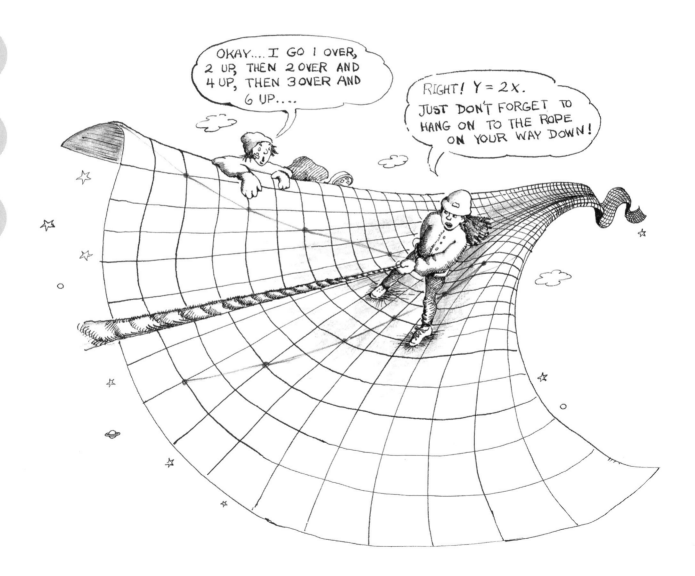

How

• Look at the graph. To make a list of points on the graph, find a point and record the x and the y value. Record this information for six or seven points.

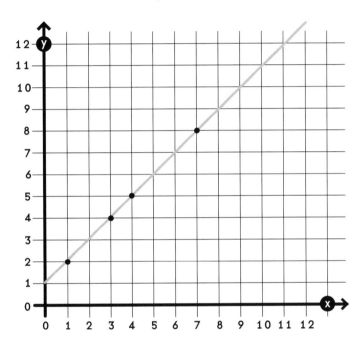

x	y
1	2
3	4
4	5
7	8
.	.
.	.
.	.

• Study the table to see if you can find the rule or equation for the graph. What do you do to x to get y?

• Look at Graph A on the graph sheet. Make a table of points for it. What's unusual about these points? When x and y are always the same, the rule or equation is x = y.

• Try the other graphs or some of your own. Make a table of the points. Find the rule or equation for the graph.

• Be ready to share how you came up with the rules to match the graphs.

Graphs to Equations

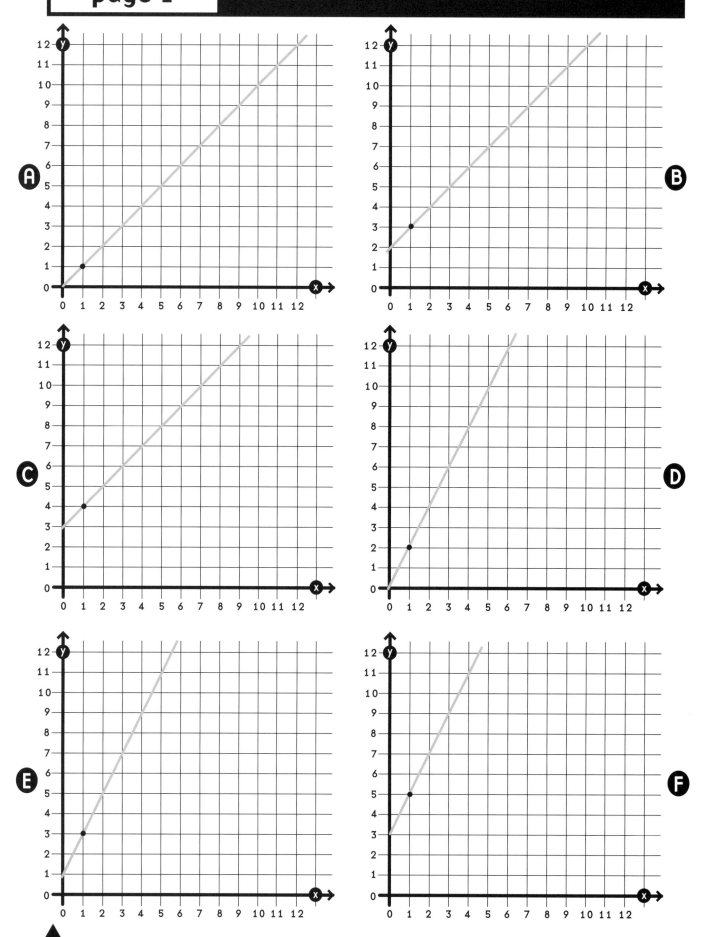

EQUALS: *FAMILY MATH—The Middle School Years*

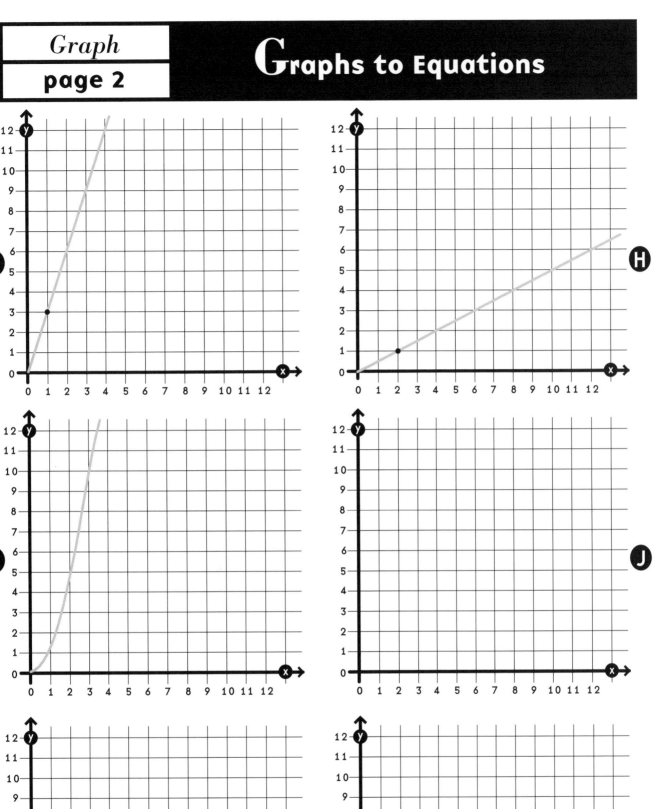

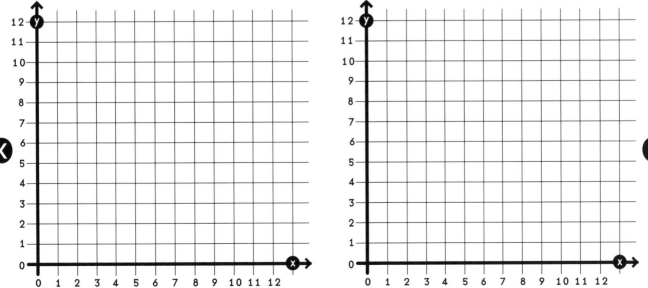

Area and Perimeter —Rectangles

Area and perimeter are important topics in middle school mathematics. Looking at them together can lead to some interesting patterns.

This activity provides a concrete method of finding the *factors* (A *factor* of a number is a whole number that divides the number evenly.) of a number. When you list all the dimensions of the rectangles for a particular area or number, you have found all of that number's factors. This area model for multiplication is extremely helpful in algebra. Looking for patterns in data is a very important aspect of the application of mathematics in everyday problems, such as ordering inventory for a shoe store.

How

• Discuss how to recognize a rectangle with your group. Is a square a rectangle? Why or why not?

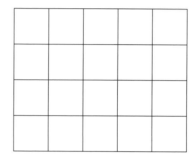

• Draw a rectangle of any size on a piece of grid paper. Count the squares to determine its *area*.

• To find the *perimeter* (the boundary line of a figure), count one unit for each side of a square that is on the outside of the rectangle.

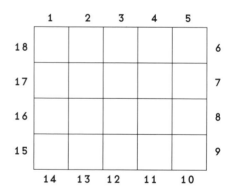

Share your results with the others in your family or group.

• Were there any rectangles with the same area? The same perimeter?

• Were there any rectangles that had the same area, but different perimeters?

• Were there any rectangles that had the same perimeter, but different areas?

• If there weren't, do you think it's possible to find examples for the last two questions?

MATERIALS

grid paper and scissors

masking tape and marking pens

adding machine tape

WHAT'S THE MATH?

Factors; area and perimeter; area model of multiplication; generalizing patterns.

• Work with your group to draw as many different rectangles as you can on grid paper for each area from 1 through 50 square units. Limit yourselves to rectangles with length and width that are whole numbers. To save space, you can say that a 4 by 5 rectangle is the same as a 5 by 4 rectangle, etc. (After all, if you rotate a 4 by 5 rectangle, it will match a 5 by 4 rectangle exactly. A mathematician would say that they are *congruent*.)

• Cut out one example of each different rectangle you find for each area and post them below the numbers on adding machine tape.

1	2	3	4	5 ...

• Study the rectangles on the tape as a group. Do you see any patterns?

• Do all the areas have the same number of rectangles?

• Are there any squares?

• Are there some areas that have only one rectangle?

• How do these areas relate to *prime numbers,* numbers that can be divided evenly only by themselves?

• Why do you think you get these results?

Area and Perimeter —Rectangles

Looking for Perimeter Patterns
• Make a chart that shows the shortest and longest perimeter for areas 1-30.

AREA IN SQUARE UNITS	SHORTEST PERIMETER	SKETCH	LONGEST PERIMETER	SKETCH
1	4	☐	4	☐
2	6	☐☐	6	☐☐
3	8	☐☐☐	8	☐☐☐
4 ⋮	8 ⋮	⊞	10 ⋮	☐☐☐☐

• The pattern of **longest** perimeters seems fairly regular. How could you figure out the longest perimeter for a rectangle with area 50 square units? Can you do this without actually making the rectangle? What about the longest perimeter for an area of 100 square units? An area of 500 square units?

• How would you describe what is happening for the **shortest** perimeters? What causes the irregularities? What do you notice when you look at all of the rectangles for a particular area?

• Which areas have the **same** shortest and longest perimeters? For example, look at the shortest and longest perimeters for area 3. How can you predict which areas will have the same longest and shortest perimeters?

Extensions

• Predict and check which number or numbers have the most rectangles for areas 50 to 100.

• How do you explain the results?

Leader Notes

• Divide the class into groups of 4 to 6. Assign each group several numbers (areas) to prepare for the chart according to the size of the class and the total numbers you want to cover. Check to see that each group understands the definitions of area and perimeter, and knows that a square is a special type of rectangle (one with all sides the same length).

• Give families grid paper and adding machine tape, so they can make their own complete number lines at home. ■

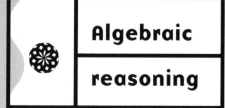
Polyomino Puzzle Square

This activity involves the recognition of congruent shapes. Two figures are *congruent* if they are exactly the same shape and size, that is if you can flip, rotate, or move one figure so that it fits exactly on the other. This activity provides materials for *Area and Perimeter—Polyominoes.*

MATERIALS

scissors

paper squares or square tiles

cardboard or heavy paper with a grid

WHAT'S THE MATH?

Spatial reasoning; geometry.

How

• Cut out a square from cardboard or heavy paper.

• Cut out a *domino* shape, that is, the shape of two squares that are completely connected together on one side.

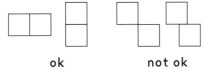

ok   not ok

• Next, cut out shapes made up of three squares—called *trominoes*. Use squares or tiles to help you find trominoes. Remember, each square must share a full side with one of the other squares.

• How many different trominoes can you find? For this activity, if two shapes can fit exactly on top of each other, we will say they are the same. Mathematicians call these shapes *congruent*. Cut out one of each of the different trominoes you find.

• Now work with four squares to make as many *tetrominoes* as you can. Work with your family to see how many different ones you can find. Cut these out of cardboard or heavy paper.

• At this stage you should have a total of nine pieces: one square and eight other polyominoes.

A *polyomino* is a group of squares connected together in such a manner that each square shares at least one full side with at least one other square.

• Put aside the long straight tetromino. Put the other eight polyomino pieces together to form a five by five square. ■

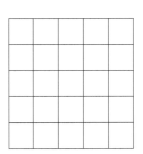

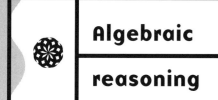
Area and Perimeter —Polyominoes

The concepts of area and perimeter in this activity are important not only in the middle grades, but in geometry, trigonometry, and calculus, as well as on the job in building and engineering. Making generalizations about these measurements requires algebraic thinking.

Have you ever thought about what happens if you start with a fixed area and rearrange its parts to make other shapes? Will the perimeter be the same for all of the new arrangements? What if you start with a fixed perimeter? Will the area change when you make different shapes with the same perimeter?

How

• How would you explain what area is? What perimeter is? See if you can agree on definitions for area and perimeter with your family and table group. Rather formal explanations might sound like this: the *area* of a two-dimensional figure is the number of square units that cover its interior; the *perimeter* of this figure is the distance around it or the distance along its boundary measured in units.

Constant Area

• First we will look at what happens to perimeter when we start with a fixed or constant area. The tetrominoes from the *Polyomino Puzzle Square* each have an area of four square units. What would you predict for their perimeters?

• Find the perimeters of the five tetrominoes and record your results. Are all of the perimeters the same? Are you surprised?

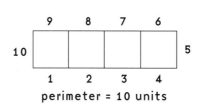

perimeter = 10 units

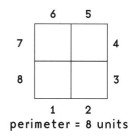

perimeter = 8 units

• Find the perimeters of the domino and two trominoes from the Polyomino Puzzle Square. Record the results.

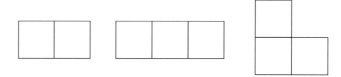

• Each *pentomino* is made up of five connected squares and has an area of five square units. Make a set of pentominoes or use those from the *Pentasquare Activities* on page 188 of the original *FAMILY MATH* book.

MATERIALS

pieces from *Polyomino Puzzle Square*

pencil and paper

scissors

WHAT'S THE MATH?
Area; perimeter; comparison of perimeters with fixed areas; comparison of areas with fixed perimeters; generalizing patterns.

• Find and record the perimeters of the 12 pentominoes.

SHAPE	PERIMETER
	12
	12 · · ·

• Discuss all of your findings.

Constant Perimeter
• Let's explore what happens when we have a constant or fixed perimeter.

• Do any of the polyominoes with different areas have the same perimeter? How many different-sized polyominoes can you find with a perimeter of 10? What about larger perimeters?

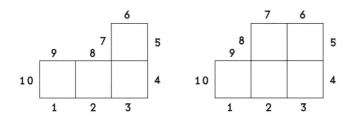

• You can go beyond pentominoes and look at polyominoes with areas of 6, 7, 8, 9, or more square units. Work with your family and group to make a chart of the perimeters for polyominoes with areas of 1 through 6 square units. Use the information you collected before.

• Study your chart to find the longest and shortest perimeters for each area. What can you say about the shapes that have the shortest perimeters? The longest?

Area and Perimeter —Polyominoes

• Use this information to help you find the shortest and longest perimeters for polyominoes with areas of 16, 20, 30, 49, 99, and 100 square units.

• Work to find a way to describe how you make the polyomino with the shortest perimeter for any area. Do the same for the longest perimeter. Mathematicians call these answers solutions for the *general case*.

One of the most important aspects of algebra is being able to find a generalization of a problem, that is a way to find the solution no matter the numbers involved. Finding the longest and shortest or maximum and minimum values in problems is a major topic in calculus with applications such as setting product prices to maximize profits. ■

Area and Perimeter of Polyominoes

AREA	SHAPE	PERIMETER	SHORTEST PERIMETER FOR AREA	LONGEST PERIMETER FOR AREA
1		4	4	4
2		6	6	6
3		8		
3		8		
4		10		10
4 .⋮		8 .⋮	8	

Growing Squares

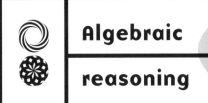

What do we mean when we say something is twice or three times as big as something else? This activity will help clarify the question as well as let us use precise mathematical language.

MATERIALS

100 or more small squares of uniform size

pencil and paper

WHAT'S THE MATH?

Area; ratios; recognizing and generalizing patterns.

How

• Lay out a sequence of squares as illustrated.

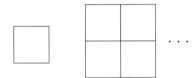

. . .

• Record the side length and area of each square in the sequence.

SIDE LENGTH IN UNITS	AREA IN SQUARE UNITS
1	1
2	4
3	.
.	.
.	.

• The second square has sides that are twice as long as the first; the third square has sides that are three times as long as the first, and so on. What happens to the area of the squares as the sides increase in length?

• Study the results with your family and table group. Do they surprise you? Can you find a pattern?

• Discuss with your group what words or sketches you would use to explain to someone else what happens to the area of a square as the sides increase. Be ready to share your ideas with other groups. ■

Extension

• Graph side length versus area for the squares you have made.

• Compare the results from this activity to those of *Growing Cubes*.

Discuss what you observe.

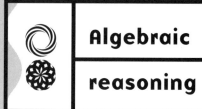
Growing Cubes

This activity explores 3-dimensional figures. What happens when you double the length of a cube? Does the volume double? What happens to the surface area?

Volume *is the number of cubic units in a solid shape. The volume of the shape below is 8 cubic units.*

Surface area *is the number of square units it takes to cover the outside of a solid shape. The surface area of the shape is 24 square units.*

Volume and surface area increase at different rates. Volume is proportional to weight, increases much more rapidly than area, and is proportional to strength.

This fact affects how large animals can be. The land-dwelling dinosaurs were at the upper limit of size for land-dwelling animals.

How

• Ask each person in your group to build a shape out of the cubes. Count the number of small cubes in each shape to determine its volume. Compare the volumes.

• Lay out a sequence of the cubes: the first with one unit on a side (just one of the small cubes); the second with two units on a side; the third with three units on a side; and so on.

• Record the side length, volume, and surface area of each cube-shape in the sequence.

SIDE LENGTH IN UNITS	VOLUME IN CUBIC UNITS	SURFACE AREA IN SQUARE UNITS
1	1	6
2	⋮	⋮
⋮		

• Look for patterns in your results. Do they surprise you? Discuss what you think is happening with a family member. Do you think the same thing will happen with other solid shapes like rectangular towers?

• Explore the last question by building a different shape to be first in the sequence. Continue the sequence. Build the second so that each side is double the length of the first; the third with sides three times the length of the first; and so on.

• Record the side length, volume, and surface area of each shape in the sequence.

• Discuss your observations with a partner. ■

MATERIALS

200-400 inch or 2-cm cubes
paper and pencil

WHAT'S THE MATH?

Volume; surface area; ratios;
generalizing patterns.

Extension

• Graph the length versus volume
and length versus surface area
for each sequence of cubes and
other shapes you have made.

How do the graphs help you
understand what happens when
the linear dimensions of a solid
are increased?

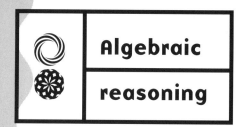
Twice as Big and More

It's not hard to find a number that is "twice as big" as another. Ten is twice as big as five; 40 is twice as big as 20. This activity will look at finding rectangles, squares, and towers of blocks that are twice as big (and more) as the original. The results might surprise you.

MATERIALS

pencil and grid paper

paper squares or cubes

scissors and calculators

WHAT'S THE MATH?

Area; volume; square root; cube root; ratios.

How

Rectangles – Twice as Big
• Draw and cut out a 3 by 2 rectangle. *Area* is the number of square units in a figure. What is the area of the 3 by 2 rectangle?

• Draw any rectangle that is twice as big — one that has twice as much area. Compare your rectangle with those your family and table group made. Are they the same? Do they all have the same area? If there are different areas, ask each person how they made their new rectangle. What accounts for these differences? Is there one right answer?

• Start with a new rectangle and make a rectangle twice as big as that one. Compare your rectangle with those your family and table group made. Ask each person how they came up with the rectangle that is twice as big as the original.

Rectangles – Three Times as Big
• Start with a 3 by 2 rectangle. Make a rectangle that has three times the area. Compare your rectangle with those your family and table group made. Are the areas the same? Discuss how everyone came up with their rectangles.

• Start with a new rectangle and make a rectangle that is three times as big. Compare your rectangle with those that your family and table group made. Discuss how everyone came up with their rectangles.

Rectangles – Four Times as Big
• Start with a 3 by 2 rectangle. Make a rectangle that has four times the area. Compare your rectangle with those your family and table group made. Are they the same? Discuss how everyone came up with their rectangles.

• Start with a new rectangle and make a rectangle that is four times as big. Compare your rectangle with those your family and table group made. Discuss how everyone came up with their rectangles.

Twice as Big and More

The square root of a number is the number that when multiplied by itself gives the original number. For example the square root of nine is 3: 3 x 3 = 9.

Squares

• Start with a 3 by 3 square. What is its area?

• What happens when you try to make a square that has twice the area? Can you find a square that has close to twice the area of a three by three square?

Math Note-Doubling the Size of the Square.

To make a square with twice the area of the 3 by 3 square, you cannot add or multiply any whole number or fraction to the original length. However, if you multiply the length of each side by the square root of 2 ($\sqrt{2}$), you will get a square that is twice as large as the original.

The area of a 3 by 3 square is 9. The area of a square that is $\sqrt{2}$ x 3 by $\sqrt{2}$ x 3 is

$$\sqrt{2} \text{ x } 3 \text{ x } \sqrt{2} \text{ x } 3$$

or

$$\sqrt{2} \text{ x } \sqrt{2} \text{ x } 3 \text{ x } 3$$

$$\sqrt{2} \text{ x } \sqrt{2} \text{ x } 9.$$

or

Since $\sqrt{2}$ x $\sqrt{2}$ = 2, the area of this new square is 2 x 9 or twice as much as the area of the original square.

The date of the discovery of $\sqrt{2}$ is uncertain. Some historians believe the Hindus knew of this number; others say the Babylonians did work that would have led to the discovery of $\sqrt{2}$.

The followers of Pythagoras, who belonged to a secret society in Greece, believed all numbers could be expressed as ratios of whole numbers, or rational numbers. *Consequently, they found the idea of* irrational numbers *(numbers that cannot be expressed as the ratio of two whole numbers) very disturbing and swore their members to secrecy about the "dread fact." One historian wrote, "It was certainly unfortunate for the character who did leak the news: his colleagues took him out to sea for a one-way trip." Other historians say this statement is an exaggeration.*

• What do you think you will need to do to get a square that is three times as large as your original?

• What happens when you try to find a square that has four times the area of a 2 by 2 square? Four times the area of a 3 by 3 square? What can you say about quadrupling the area of a square?

• Compare the area of a 1 by 1, 2 by 2, 3 by 3, and a 4 by 4 square. How much larger is each square than the next smaller one? Is there a pattern in the increase of area?

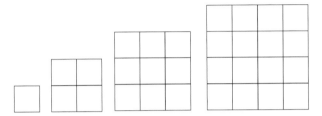

Rectangular Towers – Twice as Big
• Make a tower of blocks that is one block deep, two blocks wide, three blocks high: a 1 by 2 by 3 rectangular solid. *Volume* is the number of cubic units in a solid. What is the volume of your 1 by 2 by 3 tower?

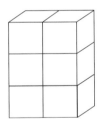

• Make a tower that has double the volume of the 1 by 2 by 3 tower. How does your tower compare to those your table group made? Experiment doubling the volume of other rectangular towers.

Rectangular Towers – Three Times as Big
• Make a tower that has triple the volume of the 1 by 2 by 3 tower. How does your tower compare to those your table group made? Experiment tripling the volume of other rectangular towers.

Twice as Big and More

The cube root of a number is the number that when multiplied by itself three times gives the original number; for example the cube root of eight is 2: 2 x 2 x 2 = 8.

Cubes

• Start with a 4 by 4 by 4 cube-shaped tower. What is its volume?

• What happens when you try to make a cube that has twice the volume? Can you find a cube that has close to twice the volume of a 4 by 4 by 4 cube?

Math Note-Doubling the size of a cube

At first it seems as if you cannot find a cube that has double the volume of a 4 x 4 x 4 cube. In fact, there are **no** whole number or fractional dimensions that work. However, if you multiply the length of each side by the cube root of 2 ($\sqrt[3]{2}$) you will have a cube that is twice as large as the original.

The volume of a 4 by 4 by 4 cube is 64 cubic units.
The volume of a cube that is

$$\sqrt[3]{2} \text{ x 4 by } \sqrt[3]{2} \text{ x 4 by } \sqrt[3]{2} \text{ x 4}$$

is twice as large because

$$\sqrt[3]{2} \text{ x 4 } \text{ x } \sqrt[3]{2} \text{ x 4 } \text{ x } \sqrt[3]{2} \text{ x 4}$$
$$= \sqrt[3]{2} \text{ x } \sqrt[3]{2} \text{ x } \sqrt[3]{2} \text{ x 4 x 4 x 4}$$

or

$$\sqrt[3]{2} \text{ x } \sqrt[3]{2} \text{ x } \sqrt[3]{2} \text{ x 64.}$$

Since $\sqrt[3]{2}$ x $\sqrt[3]{2}$ x $\sqrt[3]{2}$ = 2, the volume is 2 x 64 or twice as much as the volume of the original cube.

• What do you think you will need to do to get a cube that has a volume that is three times as large as your original?

• Compare the volumes of a 1 by 1 by 1 cube, a 2 by 2 by 2 cube and a 3 by 3 by 3 cube. How much larger is each cube than the next smaller one?

Is there a pattern in the increase of volume? ■

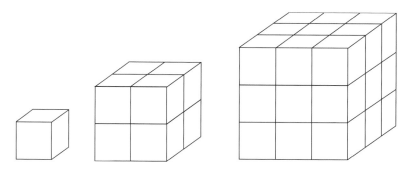

The Zero Board Game

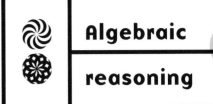
How

• Discuss negative numbers at your table. What are they? How do you explain them? What examples do you know of from everyday life? Be ready to share your ideas with other groups.

Some typical examples are temperatures that go below zero and altitudes that go below sea level or zero.

• One way to think of negative numbers is on a number line. The *positive numbers* extend to the right of zero. The *negative numbers* extend to the left of zero. Zero is neither positive nor negative.

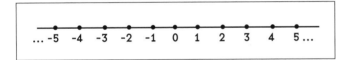

... -5 -4 -3 -2 -1 0 1 2 3 4 5 ...

Note: If you don't see a symbol in front of a number (either ⁻ or ⁺), you can assume it is positive. The negative numbers always need a negative (⁻) sign.

The Chinese indicated positive and negative numbers with different colors of counting rods.

The first known systematic treatment of negative numbers was by Bhramagupta, who lived in India from 598 to around 665.

The term *integers* refer to all of the positive and negative whole numbers and 0.

Do you remember your first or second grade teacher saying, you always have to subtract a smaller number from a larger one? "You can't do problems like 12 – 15 or 6 – 10." The teacher should have said, "You haven't learned how to do that type of problem yet." One of the key ideas in algebra is the concept of *negative numbers*. It allows us to find answers for problems like 12 – 15. This activity demonstrates how these problems work.

MATERIALS
Zero Board Game
  Number Lines
dice and markers

WHAT'S THE MATH?
Addition and subtraction of positive integers.

The Zero Board Game

NO MATTER HOW MUCH I EAT, I'M ALWAYS LEFT WITH THIS EMPTY FEELING!

The Game

• Work in groups of two to four.

• Give each group a *Zero Game Number Line.* Use only the numbers from ⁻12 to ⁺12.

• Pick a different color marker for each player.

• Start with all markers on zero.

• Take turns rolling one die until each person has had seven turns.

• On each turn, you may either add (move your marker to the right on the number line) or subtract (move your marker to the left on the number line) the number of spaces equal to the roll of the die.

• Your goal is to be the person **on** or **closest** to zero at the end of the game.

• Play several times and then discuss what you think the best strategy is for the game.

• Can you explain how you get the answers for problems like 12 − 15 and 6 − 10? ∎

Extension

• Play with boards that go from ⁻20 to ⁺20. Use two dice.

The Zero Board Game

Cut out the strips. Tape them together to make number sequences that go from −20 to +20.

+20 +19 +18 +17 +16 +15 +14 +13 +12 +11

+10 +9 +8 +7 +6 +5 +4 +3 +2 +1

0

−1 −2 −3 −4 −5 −6 −7 −8 −9 −10

−11 −12 −13 −14 −15 −16 −17 −18 −19 −20

+20 +19 +18 +17 +16 +15 +14 +13 +12 +11

+10 +9 +8 +7 +6 +5 +4 +3 +2 +1

0

−1 −2 −3 −4 −5 −6 −7 −8 −9 −10

−11 −12 −13 −14 −15 −16 −17 −18 −19 −20

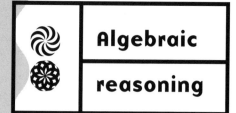
The Zero Game

Do you remember being told when you were young that you can't subtract a larger number from a smaller one? You were told that problems like 24 – 64 "didn't have an answer." Mathematicians don't like to have problems like these that don't have solutions. Eventually someone usually works out a system that provides an answer. In this case, it was the system of *negative numbers* (numbers that are less than zero) that provided the answer. (You may want to try *The Zero Board Game* before you do this activity.)

The term *integers* refers to all of the positive and negative whole numbers and 0.

How

• Discuss how to solve problems like 10 – 32 and 24 – 64, or 2 – 6 at your table.

You might think of the larger number as what someone owes on a bill and the smaller what has just been paid off. How would you figure what is left to pay? In this example, mathematicians would put a negative sign in front of the numbers that indicate that someone still owes money.

In the Zero Board Game, you moved to the left on a number line for subtraction. For 2 – 6, you would start on 2 and count 6 places to the left, landing on ⁻4.

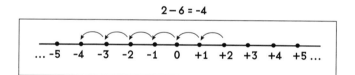

$$2 - 6 = -4$$

• Make sure everyone in the group has a way to find answers for this kind of problem before you start the game.

The Zero Game

• Work in groups of 2 to 5.

• Take turns spinning the spinner twice for each turn. Each person will have seven turns.

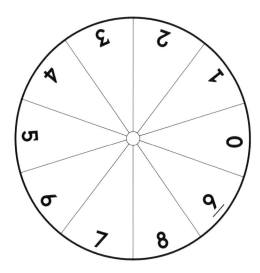

Hold a pencil point through a paper clip
at the center of the spinner and spin.

• The first number you spin on a turn goes in the tens place for a two-digit number, and the second goes into the ones place. For example, if you spin a 5 and then a 7, your number for that turn is 57.

• Everyone spins on the first round to get a starting score.

• On each succeeding turn, you may either add your new two-digit number or subtract it from your score.

• Your goal is to have a final number, positive or negative, closest to zero at the end of the seven turns.

• Play several times and then discuss good strategies for the game. ■

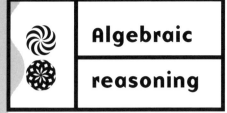
The Zero Marker Games

Suppose you owe a friend a dollar and you pay it back. Now you have no debt. The dollar you owed plus the dollar you paid results in no debt — a debt of zero dollars. Physicists and astronomers express a similar idea when they talk about antimatter. They believe that when something called an antiparticle collides with a regular particle, the result is no particles. These ideas relate to the addition of positive and negative numbers in algebra.

The term integers refer to all of the positive and negative whole numbers and 0.

The relationship between positive and negative numbers is a key concept in algebra. Numbers like +4 and -4, +32 and -32 are often called *opposites* or *additive inverses* in algebra because their sum is zero. Adding or subtracting one to the other makes zero.

How

• In the game you have two colors of markers; for example, red and blue. Whenever you have a pair of one red and one blue marker, you can treat it as if it were a zero and remove it from your playing area. In algebra, we write $^+1 + {}^-1 = 0$, or $^+2 + {}^-2 = 0$, and so on.

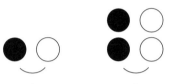

together = 0   together = 0

Note: If you don't see a symbol in front of a number (either – or +) you can assume it is positive. The negative numbers always need – signs.

• You can also add pairs (of each color) whenever you want because each pair is worth zero and adding zero to a number doesn't change the number.

Subtracting positive and negative numbers is an important skill that is developed in algebra and used in many higher mathematics and science courses.

The Zero Marker Addition Game *provides an opportunity to explore what happens when positive and negative numbers that are not opposites are added.*

The Zero Marker Subtraction Game *reinforces what happens when positive and negative numbers are subtracted. Applications occur in ship building, navigation, surveying, and working with electricity.*

MATERIALS

dice

two colors of markers

WHAT'S THE MATH?

Addition and subtraction of integers; concept of opposites or additive inverses.

The Zero Marker Addition Game

• Work in groups of 2 to 5.

• Give each person about 60 markers of two different colors, 30 of each color. Start with no markers in your playing area.

• Take turns rolling three dice until each person has had seven turns.

• On each turn, take the sum of the dice in either of the colors. You can change colors on each new turn, but you can't mix colors on one turn. Put the markers in your playing area in front of you.

• The goal is to end with no (zero) markers of one color or the fewest markers after seven turns.

• Remember, you can take out pairs of one of each color when it's your turn at any point in the game, because one marker of one color "added" to one of the other color equals zero.

• Play several times and then discuss the best strategies for the game.

The Zero Marker Subtraction Game

• Work in groups of 2 to 5.

• Give each person about 60 markers of two different colors, 30 of each color. Start with five markers of each color in your playing areas.

• Take turns rolling three dice until each person has had seven turns.

• On each turn, you must take away, subtract, the number of markers indicated by the sum of the dice in **one** of the colors. If there are not enough of the color you want to subtract, remember you can add pairs of one of each color at any point in the game from your stash in order to have enough markers of the color you want to subtract.

• You can change colors you subtract on each new turn; but you can only subtract one color on each turn.

• The goal is to end with no (zero) markers of either color or the fewest markers.

• Play several times and then discuss the best strategies for the game. ■

EXAMPLE:
Player A has 2 black markers and wants to subtract 5.

She takes 3 "zeroes".

Now she has 5 black and 3 white markers. She subtracts 5 black markers leaving 3 white markers.

ALGEBRA: WHAT'S IT ALL ABOUT?

Many adults don't remember much about algebra other than:
It has lots of x's and y's and equations.
There are rules solving equations.
It's just arithmetic using letters together with numbers.

There is more . . .

I. Algebra uses letters to represent unknown quantities or variables. The letters x and y are used most often to represent variables.

Remember problems like

$5 + \boxed{} = 7$. What is $\boxed{}$?

Algebraically we would write: $5 + x = 7$; solve for x.

II. Algebra uses basic arithmetic operations—addition, subtraction, multiplication, division—as well as square roots and exponents in equations and expressions that have both letters and numbers. Algebra uses the familiar signs, + for addition and – for subtraction; but the signs for multiplication and division are different to avoid confusion with other algebraic symbols.

For example, in arithmetic we write
$$3 \times 7 \text{ and } 105 \div 5.$$
In algebra, we write $3 \cdot 7$ and $105/5$ or $\dfrac{105}{5}$,

replacing the times sign with a dot and the division sign with a slash or horizontal bar. Placing a number immediately next to a letter also means to multiply in algebra: 3y means 3 times y.

In elementary school we learned how to add numbers like $25 + 40 = 65$ and to multiply numbers like $6 \times 48 = 288$; in algebra we use symbols as well as numbers to do arithmetic. For example, $3 \cdot x \cdot x + 4x + 2x + 1 = 3x^2 + 6x + 1$.

III. Algebra teaches techniques to solve equations and find unknown quantities.

What is often called the balance-scale model gives us an idea of how solving equations works. Think of an equation as if it were sitting on a balance scale with the equals sign at the balance point.

For example, suppose we have $5x + 4 = 19$. We start out with the scale in balance, and we must keep it that way. We could use x's in the drawing, but it's easier use physical objects. Imagine the x's as cubes; each cube represents one x. Imagine beans as numbers; each bean represents 1.

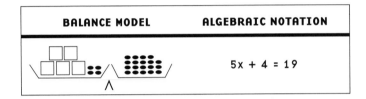

BALANCE MODEL	ALGEBRAIC NOTATION
	$5x + 4 = 19$

We want to move things around until we can figure out the unknown. But we must keep the scale in balance as we work. First we will remove four beans from each side.

BALANCE MODEL	ALGEBRAIC NOTATION
	$5x + 4 - 4$ $= 19 - 4$ $5x = 15$

Now there are 15 beans on the right side. That is, 15 beans balance 5 cubes. If we divide each side by 5, we find that one cube balances 3 beans.

BALANCE MODEL	ALGEBRAIC NOTATION
	$\dfrac{5x}{5} = \dfrac{15}{5}$ $x = 3$

We can check by looking at the equation and substituting 3 for x: $5x + 4 = 19$. We get $5 \cdot 3 + 4 = 19$, which is correct.

IV. Algebra allows us to set up equations to describe and solve problems.

Here is a typical beginning algebra problem. Bob is twice as old as Maria; together their ages add to 21. How old is each person? To solve the problem let's suppose x = Maria's age. The arithmetic can be easier if we choose x to be the smallest of a series of related unknown numbers or quantities. Here we know that Maria is younger than Bob, so we let x stand for Maria's age.

The problem gives these facts. Bob's age is twice Maria's age or 2x. The total of their ages is 21. Now we can write the algebra:

$$2x + x = 21$$
$$3x = 21$$

Dividing by 3 $\qquad x = 7$

Maria is 7 years old and Bob, who is twice as old, is 14 years old.

V. Algebra uses symbols to compare quantities.

Algebra uses special symbols to tell us whether a quantity is the same (=), greater than or equal to (>), greater than (>), less than or equal to (<) or less than (<) another quantity. These same symbols are also used with numbers in the elementary grades. When we use any of the symbols above, except =, to compare two quantities we have written an *inequality*: $2x + 3 < 14$.

When we have the equation $5x = 10$, we can figure out that x = 2. If we know that the following inequality is true, $x + 2 < 10$, what can we say about x? We can say x represents all numbers less than 8 or the numbers {7, 6, 5, 4, 3, 2, 1, 0, -1, -2, and so on}.

VI. Algebra provides a shorthand language to record how different quantities are related mathematically.

Algebra shorthand helps us to remember mathematical facts by using formulas. Remember the formula for the area of a rectangle? $A = l \cdot w$, the area equals length times width. The formula for the area of a circle is $A = \pi r^2$. Area equals pi (3.14 or 22/7) times the radius squared.

Pi, π, *is the ratio of the* circumference *of a circle to its* diameter. *This ratio is the same no matter the size of the circle. You can approximate it by 3.14 or 22/7.*

Area = length x width
Area = l x w

$A = \pi r^2$

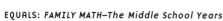

in	out
1	2
2	4
3	6
4	8

VII. Algebra provides a way to write consistent numerical patterns as equations.

Students in elementary school often see charts for "in/out machines." The first column tells the number that goes in and the second tells what number comes out; there is a consistent rule or function, that tells you what to do with the number that goes in to get the number that comes out. For the "in/out machine" to the right, the "in" number is multiplied by 2 to get the "out" number.

For this situation, the rule is multiply the input, x, by 2 to get the output, y. In algebra, we write $y = 2x$.

In algebra, we label the "in" number x and the "out" number y.

x	y
1	2
2	4
3	6
4	8
.	.
.	.
.	.
n	2n

The letter n stands for "any number."

VIII. Algebra combines with geometry to give us a way to draw equations as graphs.

For example, look at the table for $y = 2x$ in VII. We can plot the pairs of numbers for x and y, using the horizontal axis for x and the vertical axis for y. We get:

x, y
(1,2)
(2,4)
(3,6)
(4,8)
.
.
.

We can connect the points on this graph to form a line. Many relationships produce graphs that are straight lines, but others produce curves.

ALGEBRA: WHAT'S IT ALL ABOUT?

We also use tables and graphs like those shown to study data from the real world. We can use them to help us simplify various relationships. The visual aspects of these graphs often allow us to literally see patterns that were hidden when the information was in an equation or table form.

IX. The characteristics and properties of algebra are studied for themselves and as examples for how other systems, such as arithmetic, work.

One example of these ideas has to do with the *properties* of zero and one. Mathematicians are very interested in how 0 and 1 behave.

They call 0 the *identity element for addition* because no matter what number you add to zero, you get the number you started with. With similar reasoning, they call one the *identity element for multiplication* because no matter what number you multiply by one, you always get the number you started with.

Mathematicians are also very interested in the general characteristics of numbers that "turn" a given number into 0 when you add or into 1 when you multiply. For example, if you start with 5 and add ⁻5, you get 0. And when you start with 5 and multiply by ⅕, you get 1. ■

Number sense

Introduction

What do you remember from elementary school math? Most adults answer addition, subtraction, multiplication, division, fractions, percent. Some, with a groan, add word problems. A few include measuring and learning about shapes. Almost everyone mentions memorizing the multiplication tables and learning long division. In short, the focus was learning how to compute rapidly and accurately.

These skills were extremely important in the past. In the 1800s, shopkeepers paid clerks to sit on stools and do computations all day long with pen and ink. In the 1930s, the Works Progress Administration hired 500 unemployed New Yorkers to do calculations. These employees were called "computers," and were separated into four groups: addition, subtraction, multiplication, and—the elites—division. Each person worked on a part of the problem and passed the piece to another worker, according to a plan written by a senior "computer." These plans were precursors to computer programs.

> "... the majority of classrooms still rely on a traditional mathematics curriculum that, as one observer remarked, is largely composed of eight years of 15th century arithmetic, two years of 17th century algebra, and one year of 3rd century B.C. geometry."
>
> Calvin C. Moore
> Mathematics Professor
> University of California

Mathematical skills for empowerment means . . .

- developing the ability to grapple with a problem until we come to a critical understanding of it;

- learning to create as well as solve problems;

- learning to ask questions;

- learning to gather and extract useful information;

- learning to criticize assumptions;

- learning to use numbers to support or refute opinions;

- learning to cooperate and share ideas;

- placing the mathematical component of a problem in a meaningful context;

- owning all aspects of the learning experience.

Math As A Subversive Activity, Vicky Webber, *Education Links* 32, 1987-88, Australia.

Today, these skills are still necessary, but with the onset of calculators and computers, people are no longer paid to do arithmetic with pencil and paper. Doing quick and accurate mental arithmetic, estimating approximate answers, checking that calculator computations are reasonable are now very important skills. Number sense adds another dimension to basic computation that reinforces estimation and mental math.

Number Sense: What Is It?

Number sense is a quality of understanding arithmetic and numbers that is more than knowing the basic facts and methods of computation by heart.

People who have number sense use their knowledge of the relationships between numbers to help them do mental arithmetic quickly and accurately. They are good at estimating and recognizing when answers are reasonable. They have a sense of the relative size of numbers and can understand situations involving very large and very small number quantities. They use different representations for the same quantity such as 6 x 4 or 2 x 12 for 24 with ease.

This kind of understanding gives insights into problems that others think are very hard. For example, 99 x 37 can be thought of as (100 - 1) x 37 or 100 x 37 - 1 x 37, which is 3700 - 37 or 3663. Knowing you can think of 99 as 100 - 1 provides a short cut for multiplying 99 times any number. It indicates good number sense and is also a way of thinking algebraically.

Because of the developmental transition most middle school students enter during adolescence, focusing on number sense is particularly appropriate. Students are beginning to think and reason abstractly. This reasoning allows them to "step back" from their elementary school arithmetic to see the multiple ways number concepts can be used.

Knowing basic number facts, learning how to estimate, drawing pictures to represent number problems, and exploring number patterns on the calculator all contribute to the development of number sense. The following activities reinforce those key elements and improve thinking skills. ■

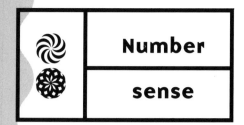
Ten, Twenty, Thirty

This activity helps to develop skills in mental arithmetic.

Being good at mental arithmetic is a valuable skill that is useful throughout life.

How

• Work in a group of two to four.

• Place the deck of cards face down on the table. Aces count one and face cards count 10.

• Turn up two cards. Place them in a row.

• Take turns drawing cards to add to the "playing" row.

• Whenever there are three cards at either end of the row, or two at one and one at the other end, that add to 10, 20, or 30, you may take those cards. Or you can draw a card from the stack and use it with two cards from one end to obtain a new sum of 10, 20, or 30.

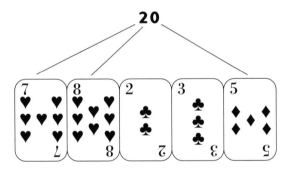

• Continue to play as long as you can take three more cards from the ends of the row.

• Play until all cards are used from the stack or there are no more plays.

• The winner is the player with the most cards at the end of the game.

Variations
• Play solitaire; you win if you have more cards than are left on the table.

• Play with jokers wild, that is, any joker can have whatever value a player wishes to assign it.

• Play with aces worth 11. ■

Carolyn Gray brought this game to FAMILY MATH. She learned it from her father.

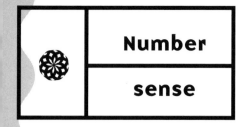

Quick Calculations

MATERIALS

counters

calculators

pencil and paper

WHAT'S THE MATH?

Mental arithmetic; shortcuts for basic operations (addition, subtraction, multiplication, and division); finding percents; understanding how numbers "go" together.

Have you ever known someone who is very quick at mental arithmetic? Thomas Fuller was such a man. He was born in Africa in 1710 and brought to America as a slave in 1724. Although he was never allowed to learn to read and write, he could do long, complicated calculations mentally.

Fuller once was asked how many seconds a man has lived who is 74 years, 17 days, and 12 hours old. Fuller took less than 90 seconds to come up with the answer. Someone else did the arithmetic with pencil and paper and got a smaller answer, but it turned out that he forgot the extra days from the leap years. Fuller was correct! Work with a partner to make your own calculation or estimate for this problem. Check the answer at the end of the activity.

Even though we all learn standard methods or algorithms for doing arithmetic in school, many people use shortcuts to make everyday calculations. This activity gives you a chance to investigate and learn some of those approaches.

How

• Talk to people at your table and in your family to find special shortcuts they use in calculating. Share any special shortcuts you use.

• Keep a record of shortcuts by topic or operation: addition, subtraction, multiplication, division, fractions, percent, and any others.

• Prepare an explanation of your favorite shortcut to share. Be ready to explain why it works. Use diagrams and examples to help make a clear presentation.

• After the presentations, decide on a new shortcut you liked and try it out in some calculations.

• Look at the hints for shortcuts on the next page. Work in pairs. Pick out a few, try them with numbers and talk about why they work. Share what you have found with your family and group.

Quick Calculations

Shortcuts for Quick Calculations

To Add Long Columns: Look for pairs and triples that add up to multiples of 10.

To Subtract: Count up from the smaller to the larger number.

To Multiply two complicated numbers: Factor each number and multiply the factors in more easy combinations; for example, $15 \times 36 = 5 \times 3 \times 3 \times 3 \times 4 = 5 \times 4 \times 3 \times 3 \times 3 = 20 \times 27 = 540$.

To Multiply by 5: Multiply by 10 and divide by 2.

To Multiply by 10: Add a zero; that is, move the decimal point one place to the right.

To Multiply by 100: Add two zeros; that is, move the decimal point two places to the right.

To Multiply by 11: Multiply by 10 and add the number.

To Multiply by 12: Multiply by 10 and add twice the number.

To Multiply by 15: Multiply by 10 and add half of that result.

To Multiply by 19: Multiply by 10 and double that answer, then subtract the number.

To Multiply by 25: Multiply by 100 and divide by 4.

To Multiply by 50: Multiply by 100 and divide by 2.

To Multiply by 52: Multiply by 100, divide by 2 and add double the number.

To Multiply by 99: Multiply by 100 and subtract the number.

To Multiply by 999: Multiply by 1000 and subtract the number.

To Multiply by 12.5 : Multiply by 100 and divide by 8.

To Multiply two numbers that differ by 2: Square the number midway between the two numbers and subtract 1.

To Multiply two numbers that differ by 3: Square one more than the smaller number and add one less than the smaller number to that result.

To Multiply two numbers that differ by 4: Square the number midway between the two and subtract 4.

To Multiply two numbers that differ by 6: Square the number midway between the numbers and subtract 9.

Shortcuts for Quick Calculations

To Multiply by ½: Divide by 2.
To Multiply by ¼: Divide by 4.
To Multiply by ¾: Divide by 4 and subtract the result from the starting number.

To Divide: Factor the divisor and dividend and cancel before dividing.

To Divide by 10: Move the decimal point one place to the left.
To Divide by 100: Move the decimal point two places to the left.
To Divide by 5: Double the number and divide by 10.
To Divide by 15: Divide by 10, double the result, and divide by 3.
To Divide by 25: Divide by 100 and multiply by 4.
To Divide by 125: Divide by 1000 and multiply by 8.

To Divide by 2½: Divide by 10 and multiply by 4.
To Divide by 12½: Divide by 100 and multiply by 8.
To Divide by 33⅓: Divide by 100 and multiply by 3.

To find 50%: Divide by 2.
To find 25%: Divide by 4.
To find 16 ⅔ %: Divide by 6.
To find 33 ⅓ %: Divide by 3.
To find 37 ½ %: Multiply by 3 and divide by 8.
To find 66 ⅔ %: Divide by 3 and subtract the result from the starting number.
To find 87 ½ %: Divide by 8 and subtract the result from the starting number. ■

The answer to Fuller's problem is 2,210,500,800 seconds.

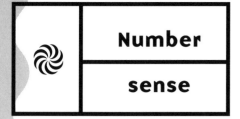

Number sense

Digit Directives:
Maximizing Multiplication

Good estimation skills can make much of mathematics easier. In this activity a little knowledge of probability will help you develop better strategies.

MATERIALS

calculators

pencil and paper

spinner with numbers 0 to 9 (page 251)

or icosahedral dice with the numbers 0–9

How

• Take turns rolling a die or spinning a spinner.

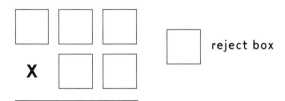

reject box

Make a copy of the multiplication problem chart as shown.

• Write the digit you roll or spin in any empty slot or the reject box.

• Your goal is to get the largest possible *product,* the answer in a multiplication problem, after six rolls.

• You cannot skip turns or move digits after they are recorded.

• After each player has completed six turns, compare the products to see which is the largest.

• Now work together to help each person in your group to rearrange their numbers to get the largest possible product.

• Do you think a calculator would help or hinder your thinking in this activity? Why? Discuss this with your family.

Variations

• Try to place the digits so that you obtain the smallest possible product. How does this variation compare with the original activity?

• Make up different problem charts for more multiplication games. ■

Digit Directives:
Diminishing Division

How

• Take turns rolling a die or spinning a spinner.

reject box

Make a copy of the division problem chart as shown.

• Write the digit you roll or spin in any empty slot or the reject box.

• Your goal is to get the smallest possible *quotient,* answer, after six rolls.

• You cannot skip turns or move digits after they are recorded.

• After each player has completed six turns, compare the quotients to see which is the smallest.

• Now work together in your group to rearrange each person's numbers to get the smallest possible quotient.

• Do you think a calculator would help or hinder your thinking in this activity? Why? Discuss this with your family.

• Write 485 ÷ 132 as 485/132. Does writing the division problem as a fraction help you choose where to place the numbers? Why or why not? ■

MATERIALS

calculators

pencil and paper

spinner with numbers 0 to 9 (page 251)

 or icosahedral dice with the numbers 0–9

WHAT'S THE MATH?

Estimation; division; probability.

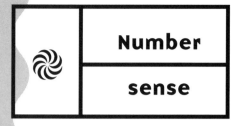

Number sense

Digit Directives:
Finding Fractions

Comparing fractions and estimating decimal equivalents quickly and accurately are useful skills in everyday life as well as in algebra and science courses such as chemistry.

How

• Work in groups of two to four.

• Remove the face cards from a deck of playing cards. The aces will represent ones.

• Take turns with your family or partner rolling an icosahedral die or spinning a 0–9 spinner to obtain 4 digits. Take a card for each digit you roll or spin. It's OK to have two or three cards with the same digit.

• Arrange the cards to form two two-digit numbers to make a fraction that is as close as possible to 1, but not greater than 1.

• Compare your fraction with those of others in the group.

• Discuss how you can tell which of two fractions is closer to 1.

• Repeat the game several more times.

• Discuss your strategies for getting a fraction as close to 1 as possible.

Variations
• Play to get the smallest possible number.

• Play to get the largest possible number.

MATERIALS

calculators

pencil and paper

playing cards

spinner with numbers 0 to 9 (page 251)
or icosahedral dice with the numbers 0 to 9

WHAT'S THE MATH?

Ordering fractions; fraction/decimal equivalents; estimation.

Extensions

- Write your numbers in boxes as you get them. You cannot skip turns or move the digits after they are recorded. The person with the fraction closest to 1 still wins. Discuss how this change in rules affects the game.

- How many different fractions are possible?

- Once you have four numbers, how many different fractions can you make? Does it make a difference if two (or three or four) of the numbers are the same? If so, in what way?

- What is the grand total when you consider all the possible groups of four numbers you could roll or spin?

Counting problems such as the one in the extensions come from the field of combinatorics (combinational math) in discrete math (math that deals with elements that can be counted). Making lists or tree diagrams are common approaches to finding the total number of possibilities. ∎

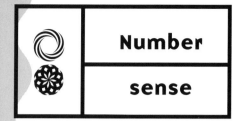
Sharing the Whole

Developing a good understanding of fractions is not only important in the middle grades, but key to future work in algebra, geometry, calculus, and the sciences.

WHAT'S THE MATH?

Fractions; parts of a whole.

How

• You want to divide a cake into equal pieces for your family and friends at a gathering. Decide how many people need a share.

• Draw a picture of the cake and sketch lines on it to indicate how you would cut it.

• Label one of the pieces with the fraction of the cake that it represents. Also indicate how many pieces of that fraction make up the whole. (For example, if there are two pieces of a cake, there are ²⁄₂ in the whole cake.)

• Share your drawing with your family and the others at your table. Is there more than one fair way to share the cake for the same-sized group? Is it easier to share the cake for a family of 2 than for a family of 3 or 5? What other family sizes make it easier to divide the cake into equal pieces? Does the shape of the dish affect how easy it is to divide the cake into equal pieces? Which shapes are easy? Which are hard?

• Pick the number of pieces you want to cut and one of the shapes from the Shape Sheet. Work together to find as many ways to cut the cake into equal-sized pieces as you can.

• Try another number and shape. Make drawings and notes to help you share your work with other groups.

• Draw new shapes to use. ■

Extension

• Find the decimal equivalent for the different fractions for the pieces you have drawn. For example, if the fraction is ½, you can find its decimal equivalent by dividing 1 by 2 by hand or on a calculator, or by using the fraction-decimal key on a fraction calculator.

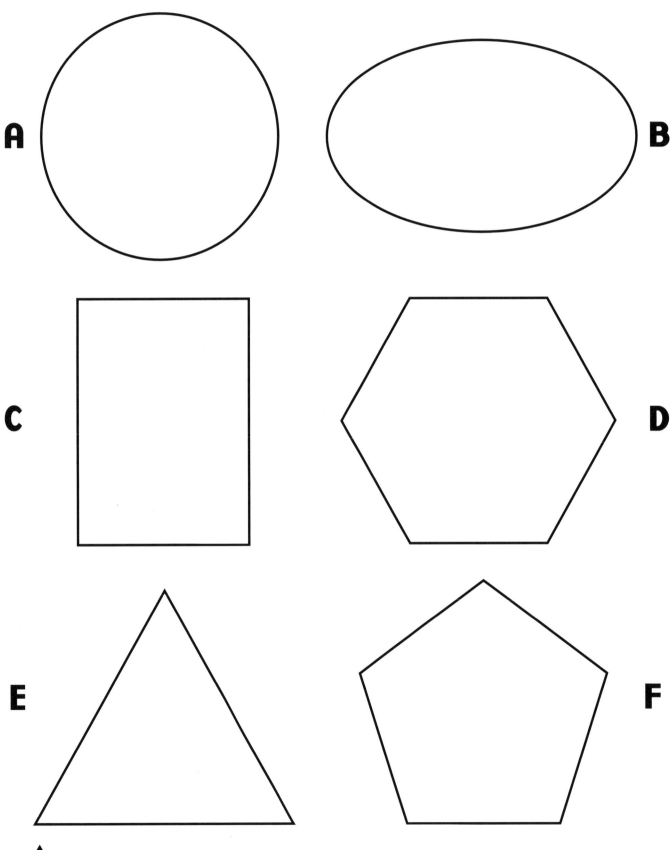

A

B

C

D

E

F

Numerous Remainders

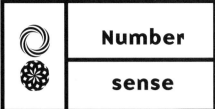

These puzzles reinforce understanding of division and help in the development of number sense. Mathematicians say these ideas are part of the field of Number Theory.

This type of puzzle was of considerable interest in ancient China. The second puzzle is an example written by Master Sun about 280 A.D. One approach to solving this type of problem is called the Chinese Remainder Theorem in recognition of Master Sun's work.

How

• Work with a partner and discuss your strategies to solve the following puzzles.

Find a number that:
has a remainder of 6 when divided by 7, and a remainder of 3 when divided by 5.

Find a number that:
has a remainder of 2 when divided by 3, a remainder of 3 when divided by 5, and a remainder of 2 when divided by 7.

Find a number that:
has a remainder of 2 when divided by 3, a remainder of 4 when divided by 5, and a remainder of 1 when divided by 7.

• What strategies did you like best? Why? Did you find more than one number that would work for any of the problems?

• Make up a new puzzle for another group. ■

MATERIALS
pencil and paper
counters, beans, or buttons

WHAT'S THE MATH?
Division and remainders; logical thinking.

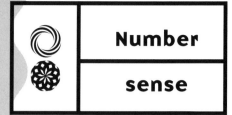
Benchmarks for Estimation: *Time*

All the zeroes in large numbers make it hard to get a sense of what they mean. Connecting them to something familiar often clarifies the situation. This activity helps to develop the aspect of number sense in connection to the measurement of time.

The term *benchmark* has come to mean a guide or something to measure by. There are so many large numbers that affect our lives, it is important to gain an understanding of their meaning and impact. A collection of benchmarks can help you do this.

WHAT'S THE MATH?

Time; large numbers; place value; estimation; proportional reasoning.

How

• Look at the number pattern below. How do you know what the next number will be? Can you name these numbers:
1; 10; 100; 1,000; 10,000; 100,000; 1,000,000; 10,000,000; 100,000,000; 1,000,000,000?

What are the names of the following numbers:
 10,000,000,000; 100,000,000,000; and 1,000,000,000,000?

• Estimate your age in seconds. Decide first if you are more or less than one million seconds old.   What about the other members of your family or group? Are they more or less than a million seconds old? More or less than a billion seconds old?

Keep notes as you work out your age in seconds to share with other groups.

• How long is one million seconds? How long is a billion seconds? A trillion seconds? Are you surprised?

How much larger is a billion than a million? A trillion than a billion?

Extension

• During the week look up some other events that happened about a billion and a trillion seconds ago. Bring them to share in the next class.

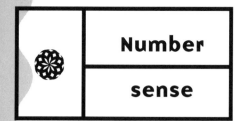
Benchmarks for Estimation: *A Million Dollars and the Cost of Living*

Is a million dollars really a lot of money? How long would it take you to earn that much? How far would it go? Starting with small numbers and building up to larger ones is a strategy that helps with estimation. Once you have found one number, you can use that as a benchmark or guideline to estimate other larger numbers.

In surveying, a *benchmark* is the point of a known elevation that surveyors use to establish other elevations.

MATERIALS	WHAT'S THE MATH?
pencil and paper	Large numbers; rates;
calculators	everyday living expenses.

How

A Million Dollars

• With your family and table groups, discuss how long it would take you to earn a million dollars.

• Suppose you worked for $5 an hour, 8 hours a day, 5 days a week for 50 weeks a year? What if you earned $15 an hour? $20,000 a year? $40,000 a year? $60,000 a year?

Cost of Living

• Could you afford to live in your own apartment if you earned $5 an hour? Could you afford a car as well? Discuss what information you would need to figure this out.

• Look in your local newspapers for information on how much studios and one-bedroom apartments rent for in your area. Who usually pays for the utilities (gas, electricity, water, and garbage)? You or the landlord? How could you find out how much they would cost each month? Check out how much a used car costs. Call an insurance company to find out how much you would have to pay for insurance. Bring the information for the next class.

• If $5 an hour is not enough to cover renting your own apartment and having a car, how much do you think you would need?

• If you decide to live at home, what would be a fair amount for you to pay for your share of food and utilities? ■

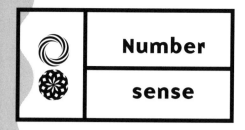

Number sense

Benchmarks for Estimation: *Apple* *and Microsoft*

Understanding large numbers and their relationships is very important in the mathematics of everyday life. Different approaches can give you benchmarks or guidelines to help you find a relationship.

A collection of guidelines, or *benchmarks*, can help you better understand the relationships of large numbers, their meaning and implications.

> In July 1997 Bill Gates of Microsoft met with Steve Jobs of Apple Computer. Gates agreed to buy $150,000,000 worth of Apple's stock.
>
> One newscaster said that was not a big investment for Bill Gates, because Microsoft is worth 190 billion dollars.

How

• Do you agree? Talk with a partner. Be ready to explain why you do or do not agree with the news commentator. Discuss what mathematics support your decision.

• Apple was worth approximately $3,100,000,000 at the time. Was Gates' contribution significant for Apple?

• If you had $100, how much would you have to give away to do the equivalent of what Gates did? Would it be a hardship for you to give that much away? Talk with your family about how to decide. ∎

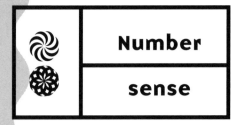
Mayan Mathematics

The Maya were one of the first peoples in the world to use the number zero and place value. These characteristics are part of what makes the decimal or base ten number system so easy in comparison to systems such as Roman numerals.

The Maya used their familiarity with factors and multiples to avoid having to use fractions. Their extraordinary precise solar, lunar, and Venus calendars demonstrate their proficiency with multiples.

You can use black beans to represent dots in the Mayan number system, sticks to represent the bars, and shells or O rings to represent zeroes. Your goal is to figure out how the Mayan number system works and to use this knowledge in a game.

How

• Work in groups of two to four.

• Each group needs about 10 beans, 10 sticks, 10 shells or O rings, a Mayan Number Spinner and a Mayan Place Value Board for each player.

• Think about the symbols we use in our number system. There are ten symbols: 0, 1, 2, 3, ..., 8, and 9. The number after 9, we call ten, is written 10. It stands for one ten and no ones. The number we call fifteen, 15, stands for one ten and five ones. What about 36? 47? 92?

• We call the number that comes after 99, one hundred. It stands for one hundred, no tens, and no ones. What about 127? 162? 568? 904?

• What happens after 999? 9,999? And so on?

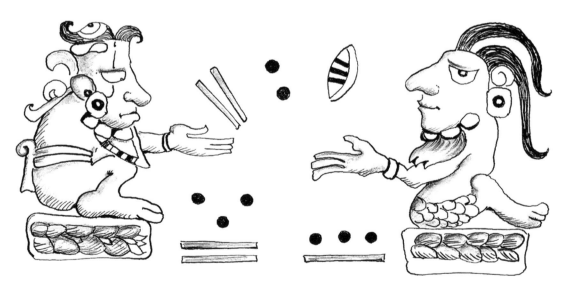

This activity was developed by Rhett Rattley-Lewis of the National Urban Coalition in 1993.

MATERIALS

popsicle sticks or other sticks

black beans and 0-rings or shells

Mayan Place Value Boards

Mayan Number Spinner

WHAT'S THE MATH?

Place value; number systems; exponents and powers.

• What if you want to use a base two number system? How many symbols do you need for base two? (Two symbols.) What would they be? (0 and 1.) You would have a one's place, 2^0; a two's place, 2^1; a four's place, 2^2; an eight's place, 2^3; a sixteen's place, 2^4; and so on. How would you write two in base two? Three? Four? Six? Twelve? Sixteen?

• What happens for base 8?

• What would happen if you wanted to work with base 11? You need a total of eleven symbols. You would need a new symbol to represent ten, because "10" stands for one eleven and no ones in base eleven.

• How many symbols do you need for base 16? How many new symbols?

The requirement for different symbols for the different digits of a number system is a practical limitation on how large a base might be. This is what makes the Mayan number system so incredible. The Mayan number system is base 20. They worked out a way to write numbers in a base 20 system with just three symbols!

The Maya use a shell to represent zero, a bean to represent one, and a stick to represent five. The symbols for these are a picture of a shell, a dot, and a bar. With these three symbols and place value, any number can be expressed. The place value in our number system increases from right to left, while the Maya's increases vertically from bottom to top, starting with a one's place, then a twenty's place, a four hundred's place, an eight thousand's place, and so on.

The ones, tens, hundreds, thousands, ten thousands, hundred thousands, millions, and so on, indicate place value in our decimal or base 10 number system.

They are all powers of 10:
$10^0 = 1$;
$10^1 = 10$;
$10^2 = 100$;
$10^3 = 1,000$,
and so on.

The small raised number, the exponent, that appears by some numbers tells you how many times to multiply that number by itself. This is called raising a number to the power of whatever the exponent is.

For example,
$10^3 = 10 \times 10 \times 10 = 1,000$,
which is 10 raised to the power of 3.

Any number to the zero power is equal to one.

For example,
$2^0 = 1$.

Base 2, base 8, and base 16 are all used in computer programming.

Mayan Mathematics

Seven in the Mayan system
is written:

Seventeen is written:

One hundred twenty is written:

Four hundred five is written:

Working with the Mayan place value system gives adults and teenagers a sense of how children feel when they are learning our number system. The disequilibrium we feel as we try to understand a base 20 system provides a glimpse into the difficulties faced by that seven-year-old trying to learn the base 10 decimal system.

• Look at your Mayan Place Value Board. Take turns putting out beans (to stand for dots), sticks (to stand for bars), and shells or O rings (to stand for zeroes) to represent the numbers one, two, three, four, five, six, seven, eight, nine, and ten in the Mayan system. What happens when you go from four to five? Is it OK to have five beans? Or should you trade them for a stick or bar?

• Continue with some larger numbers like 16, 19, 20, 24, 33, and so on. How would you show 360? 400? 720?

• When everyone in your group feels comfortable making Mayan numbers, try *The Mayan Trading Game.*

Note: the Maya changed their number system slightly for religious dates. The 400's place changed to a 360's place. This matches their calendar, which had 18 months of 20 days each . The Maya also had 5 extra days to make a 365 day year. These days were grouped as a month at the end of the year and thought to be of special danger and bad luck. The Maya also had a method to make up for the extra quarter day that occurs each year.*

The Mayan Trading Game
• Make sure each person in your group has a Mayan Number Board and 10 black beans, 10 sticks, and 10 O rings or shells. The group also needs a Mayan Number Spinner.

• Take turns spinning the Mayan Number Spinner. On your first turn make the number indicated and place it in the one's or the 20's section of the board.

• On the following turn make the number indicated and place it in the one's or 20's section. Add it to the total you have, making the appropriate trades.

• Continue until everyone has had seven turns.

• The winner is the person who comes closest to 400, but not over 400. Exactly 400 is perfect.

There are many books about the Maya. The source for this information is Number *by John McLeish published by Bloomsbury in 1991.*

Mayan Mathematics

VEGESIMAL = BASE 20

| ≡ = 0 | ● = 1 | —— = 5 |

EIGHT THOUSAND'S

FOUR HUNDRED'S

TWENTY'S

ONE'S

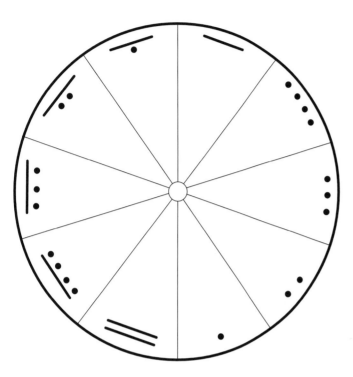

Hold a pencil point through a paper clip
at the center of the spinner and spin.

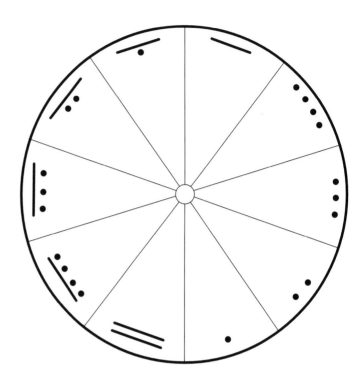

Hold a pencil point through a paper clip
at the center of the spinner and spin.

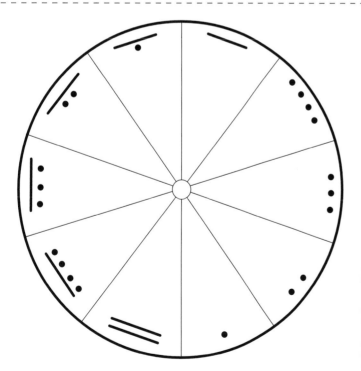

Hold a pencil point through a paper clip
at the center of the spinner and spin.

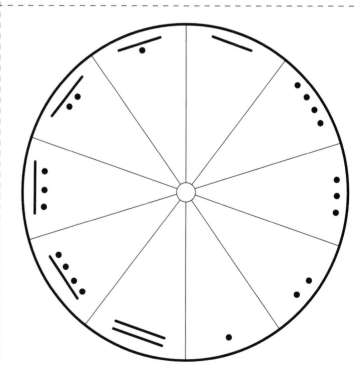

Hold a pencil point through a paper clip
at the center of the spinner and spin.

Tax Collector Exploration

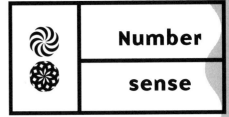

In *Tax Collector* in the original *FAMILY MATH* book, you work to beat the tax collector using paychecks from $1 through $12 or paychecks from $1 through $24. In this extension of the activity, you will explore what happens in variations of the game for the following cases: using just one $1 paycheck; $1 and $2 paychecks; $1, $2, and $3 paychecks; $1, $2, $3, and $4 paychecks, and so on, up to using $1 through $25 paychecks. Look for patterns that you can use in all the variations of the game.

Your family is about to meet the tax collector. Your family's goal is to end the meeting keeping more money than the tax collector.

Remember, the tax collector must receive a tax payment for each paycheck that your family (the taxpayer) receives. Payment is made in factors of the check you choose.

Do you think you can beat the tax collector for all of the cases listed above?

> A *factor* of a number is a whole number that divides the number evenly.

> Factors of numbers play a key role in these puzzles. Familiarity with factors is important in division, fractions, and algebra.

How

• Pick a case from the list above; that is pick the number of paychecks to use. For example, suppose you start with the case that has 14 paychecks: $1 through $14.

• Put the 14 paychecks above the tax collector board.

• Choose a paycheck for your family and put it on the taxpayer side of the board (your family's side of the board). For example, suppose you choose $10.

• Give the tax collector (put on the tax collector's side) all of the factors for your paycheck that have not been used. For $10 on the first turn, you will have to give the tax collector $1, $2, and $5. (The factor, 10, has already been used in your taxpayer column.)

MATERIALS

paycheck squares 1–25

tax collector boards

pencil and paper/calculators

WHAT'S THE MATH?

Factors; logical thinking.

Tax Collector Exploration

• If all the factors of a paycheck have been played, the tax collector gets that paycheck.

• Once a paycheck (number) has been used, it cannot be used again until the next game.

• Since 1 is a factor of every number, the tax collector will get 1 along with any other factors of the first number or paycheck that you choose.

• Continue choosing paychecks until there are no paychecks left that have factors available. The tax collector will get these leftover paychecks.

• Add your paychecks and compare your sum with that of the tax collector. Did your family beat the tax collector? If not, try several more games to see if you can beat the tax collector or until you can convince others that you cannot beat the tax collector with 14 paychecks.

• Try the other cases and keep a record of your results. Discuss the strategies you use to beat the tax collector.

• Can you win for all of the numbers of paychecks from $1 through $25? What about larger numbers? ∎

TAX COLLECTOR BOARD

Taxpayer	Tax Collector

Paycheck Numbers

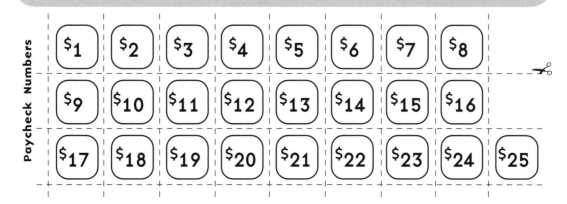

$1 $2 $3 $4 $5 $6 $7 $8

$9 $10 $11 $12 $13 $14 $15 $16

$17 $18 $19 $20 $21 $22 $23 $24 $25

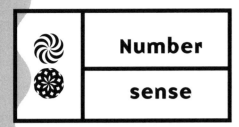

The Game of Euclid

This activity is based on the work of Euclid. Euclid was a Greek mathematician who lived around 300 B.C. He invented the type of geometry taught in high school math courses.

The game is based on a method or algorithm for finding the greatest common divisor of two numbers, that is, the largest number that will divide two given numbers.

How

• Find a partner. Decide who will go first.

• Each player chooses a whole number and records it secretly. (You might try numbers between 20 and 200 to start with; the numbers in the example are 27 and 151.)

• The two numbers are revealed and play begins.

• The first player subtracts any multiple of the smaller number from the larger that produces a difference that is greater than or equal to 0. Note, one times a number is considered a multiple of the number.

• The second player performs the same process on the new pair of numbers; that is, the original smaller number and the new number that the first player got on the first move.

• Play continues until one of the players produces a new pair of numbers where one of the numbers is 0. That player is the winner.

• Play several games. Then discuss your ideas and strategies with your partner.

• Does it matter if you are the first or second player?

• Is there a relationship between the number that is not zero in the winning pair and the two original numbers? ■

SAMPLE GAME

Start			27 & 151
Player A:	-3 x 27	27	$\frac{-81}{70}$
Player B:	-1 x 27	27	$\frac{-27}{43}$
Player A:	-1 x 27	27	$\frac{-27}{16}$
Player B:	-1 x 16	$\frac{-16}{11}$	16
Player A:	-1 x 11	11	$\frac{-11}{5}$
Player B:	-1 x 5	$\frac{-5}{6}$	5
Player A:	-1 x 5	$\frac{-5}{1}$	5
Player B:	-5 x 1	1	$\frac{-5}{0}$
B WINS			

Extensions

- Can you explain the connection of the game to greatest common divisors?

- When is it useful to know the greatest common divisor?

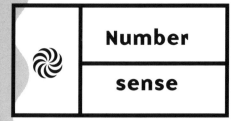

Decimal Double Digit

The *Double Digit* game is very popular in FAMILY MATH classes. This version focuses on decimal place value. Estimation and mental arithmetic are also important in this activity.

How

• Work with a partner or a small group.

• Prepare a record sheet for each person for each game.

• Take turns rolling a die. The number you roll can be written in either the tenths column or the hundredths column. The possibilities for a three are 0.30 or 0.03, for a four, 0.40 or 0.04, and so on. (When you write a number in the tenths column, you may want to write a "0" in the hundredths column to help keep the columns straight.)

• You cannot change a number after you have recorded it.

 • Each player must take seven turns.

• The person who comes closest to 1.00 without going over wins.

• After several rounds of playing competitively, work together to get the best scores for each person in the group. Discuss what strategies you think work best.

• Probability plays an important role in this game. What are the chances of rolling a 1, 2, 3, 4, 5, or 6 on the die? How does this information help you with the game? ■

RECORD SHEET		
	Tenths	Hundredths
1.	.2	0
2.	.0	4
3.		
4.		
5.		
6.		
7.		
TOTAL		

Extensions

- Look at the record sheets for one game. If each person is allowed to move one number from the tenths column to the hundredths column, or vice versa, find what move will raise each person's score the most.

- Try *Decimal Digit Cover Up*.

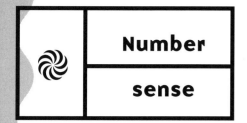

Number sense

Decimal Digit Cover Up

This activity reinforces decimal place value for tenths and hundredths. Estimation comes into play as well as ideas from probability.

MATERIALS

dice

Decimal Digit Cover Up Game Board

10 by 1 strips and 1 by 1 squares
  to match game board squares

WHAT'S THE MATH?

Addition of decimals; place value; estimation; area model for base 10; probability.

How

• Work with a partner or a small group. Each person needs a game board, 10 strips, and 15 small squares.

• The game board is one whole, 1.00. The strips are worth ten hundredths or one tenth, 0.10; they cover 10 squares on the game board. The small squares are worth one hundredth, 0.01; they cover one square on the game board.

• The goal is to cover the whole game board with tenths (strips) and hundredths (small squares) without going over the edge or overlapping any pieces.

• Each player has seven turns.

• Take turns rolling a die.

• The number you roll tells how many tenths or hundredths you can take. You cannot mix tenths and hundredths on the same turn, but can change on the next turn.

• Lay out the strips and small squares on the game board. When you get 10 hundredths (small squares), you can trade them for one tenth (a strip).

• The person who comes closest to covering the whole game board without going over wins.

• You must use all seven turns. ■

.01	.01	.01	.01	.01	.01	.01	.01	.01	.01
.01	.01	.01	.01	.01	.01	.01	.01	.01	.01
.01	.01	.01	.01	.01	.01	.01	.01	.01	.01
.01	.01	.01	.01	.01	.01	.01	.01	.01	.01
.01	.01	.01	.01	.01	.01	.01	.01	.01	.01
.01	.01	.01	.01	.01	.01	.01	.01	.01	.01
.01	.01	.01	.01	.01	.01	.01	.01	.01	.01
.01	.01	.01	.01	.01	.01	.01	.01	.01	.01
.01	.01	.01	.01	.01	.01	.01	.01	.01	.01
.01	.01	.01	.01	.01	.01	.01	.01	.01	.01

Myth: Learning mathematics requires special ability, which most students do not have.

Reality: Only in the United States do people believe that learning mathematics depends on special ability. In other countries, students, parents, and teachers all expect that most students can master mathematics if only they work hard enough. The record of accomplishments in these countries—and in some intervention programs, in the United States—shows that most students can learn much more mathematics than is commonly assumed in this country.

Everybody Counts, p.10.

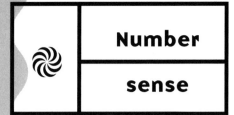
Towers

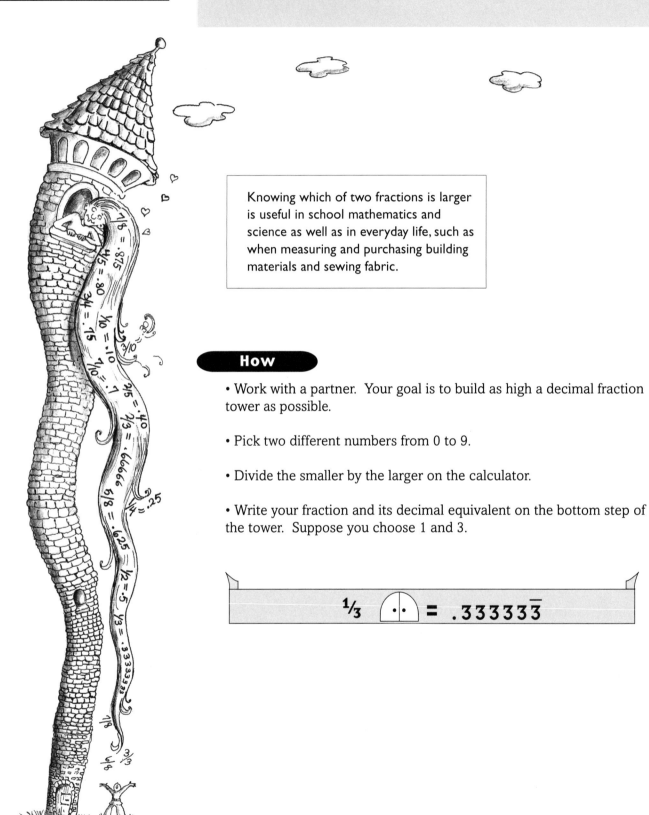

Knowing which of two fractions is larger is useful in school mathematics and science as well as in everyday life, such as when measuring and purchasing building materials and sewing fabric.

How

• Work with a partner. Your goal is to build as high a decimal fraction tower as possible.

• Pick two different numbers from 0 to 9.

• Divide the smaller by the larger on the calculator.

• Write your fraction and its decimal equivalent on the bottom step of the tower. Suppose you choose 1 and 3.

⅓ = .333333‾

MATERIALS

pencil and paper

calculators

WHAT'S THE MATH?

Ordering fractions; fraction/ decimal equivalents; multiple representations of a number.

• Now it's your partner's turn to build the second step. You want the second step fraction to be less than 1, but larger than the one on the bottom step. Suppose your partner chooses 2 and 5.

$$\frac{2}{5} = .400000$$

$$\frac{1}{3} = .333333\overline{3}$$

• Continue taking turns and adding steps until you cannot find a fraction that fits between the last step and 1.

• How high is your tower? Play several more times. Start with a new first step each time. Work to build a higher tower each time.

• Discuss your strategies for building higher towers.

Variation
• Play with a combination of double and single digits in the fractions. ■

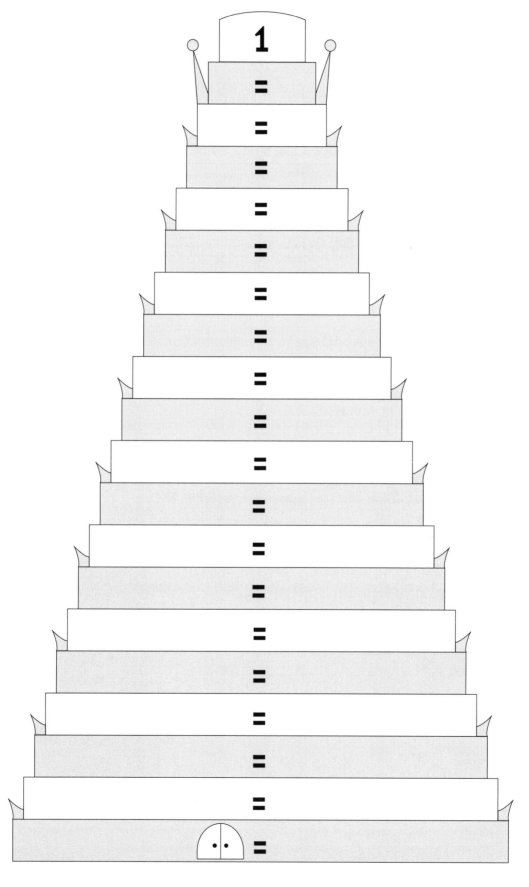

The Fraction, Decimal, Percent Connection

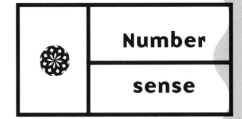

The concept of *multiple representations* is key in middle school mathematics. This refers to the idea that a number, algebraic equation, or problem can be written or expressed in a variety of equivalent ways. One example is equivalent fractions: ½ is the same as ²⁄₄, which is the same as ²⁴⁄₄₈, and so on.

This activity looks at *equivalent representations* in fraction, decimal, and percent form. There are rules to convert fractions to decimals, decimals to percents, and vice versa, with pencil and paper in almost all middle school books. This activity focuses on how a fraction calculator can help perform these tasks and provide additional information to reinforce the understanding of these skills. You might also want to try *Fraction Calculator Explorations*.

MATERIALS
pencil and paper
fraction calculators
journal for notes

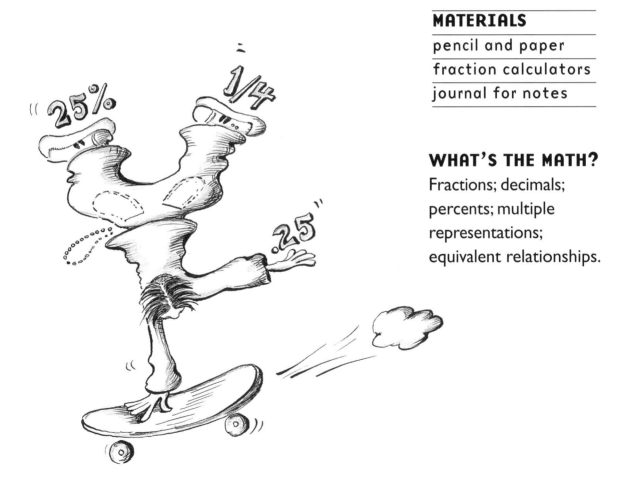

WHAT'S THE MATH?
Fractions; decimals; percents; multiple representations; equivalent relationships.

The Fraction, Decimal, Percent Connection

Terms about fractions are important to know. The *numerator* is the top number in a fraction; the *denominator* is the bottom number in a fraction. Numbers like ⁵⁄₂ are called *improper fractions*, because the numerator is larger than the denominator. Those like 2½ are called *mixed numbers*, because they contain a fraction and a whole number.

How

Fractions and Decimals

• Write some examples of fractions, decimals, and percents. What makes a fraction a fraction? A decimal a decimal? A percent a percent?

• Is ⁵⁄₂ a fraction? Is 7.85 a decimal? Can you have a percent that is greater than 100%, such as 200%? What would that mean?

• Can you think of a fraction and a decimal that are worth the same? How do you know they are the same? What about a percent and a decimal? A fraction and a percent? Some common examples are ½ = 0.5 = 50% and ¼ = 0.25 = 25%.

• Get out a fraction calculator, such as the Texas Instruments Math Explorer. Find the key with the ⬭ / ⬭ symbol. You can use this to enter fractions on the calculator. To enter ½ push a 1, then the ⬭ / ⬭ then the 2. What do you see on the screen?

• What happens when you push the ⬭F⇄D⬭ key? Do you get a number that is equivalent to ½? The ⬭F⇄D⬭ or fraction to decimal key changes the number on the display to the other form. What happens when you push the ⬭F⇄D⬭ key again? Is that fraction equivalent to ½? What happens when you push the ⬭Simp⬭ key and then = ? The ⬭Simp⬭ key simplifies or reduces the fraction in the display when you enter ⬭Simp⬭ = . Sometimes you have to use this combination several times to get the simplest form of a fraction. Why is that?

• Try some other fractions. Enter them and then change them to decimals. Can you change them all back to fractions? What happens with ⅓? ¹⁄₁₂? Do you know why?

• Make a table to record fractions and their decimal equivalents. Find out which fractions, when changed to decimals, won't change back to fractions. Is there a pattern?

Decimals, Percents, and Fractions

• To change a fraction to a decimal, divide the numerator by the denominator.

• To change a decimal to a fraction, count the number of places to the right of the decimal. Write the digits of the number as the numerator. The denominator is 10 to the number of decimal places you counted. For example,

$$.4589 = {}^{4589}\!/_{10^4} = {}^{4589}\!/_{10,000};$$
$$1.35 = {}^{135}\!/_{10^2} = {}^{135}\!/_{100}.$$

• To change a fraction to percent, divide the numerator by the denominator and move the decimal point two places to the right. For example, for ¼ , we have 1 ÷ 4 = .25; and moving the decimal point two places to the right gives 25%.

• To change a decimal to percent, you multiply by 100 and write a percent sign following the result. For example, 0.4 x 100 = 40, so 0.4 is equivalent to 40%.

• Make a table to record equivalent forms of fractions, decimals, and percents. Start with a few fractions and find their decimals and percents; then start with a few decimals and find their equivalents. Finally start with percents. ■

Percent means parts per hundred. The term originated during Roman times to express tax rates.

FRACTION	DECIMAL	PERCENT
¹/₂	0.50	50%
³/₄	0.75	75%
1 ¹/₂	1.50	150%

Fractions came about when people were trying to make more accurate measurements. First they measured using whole units, then whole units and half units. Then they added quarter units, eighths, and so on. Fractions can indicate several things: the part of a whole, a ratio that compares two quantities, or division.

Extension

• Try the *Towers* activity.

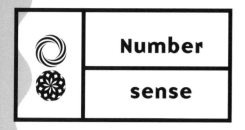
Fraction Calculator Explorations

Calculators are a common tool in the workplace today. Knowing when and how to use them is an important skill. Fraction calculators are especially amazing! With them you can explore the arithmetic of fractions and integer division, reinforce the relationships between fractions and decimals, and learn more about the order of operations, reciprocals, powers, roots, and positive and negative numbers.

This activity provides an overview of some of the unique functions of this calculator. (*Note:* You may want to try only one or two sections of this activity at a time.)

MATERIALS

fraction calculators

pencil and paper

WHAT'S THE MATH?

Fractions; decimals; fractions/decimal equivalents; improper fractions; mixed numbers; simplifying fractions; percent; multiples; integer division and remainders; powers and exponents; order of operations; unit conversions; reciprocals; square roots; other roots.

If you get stuck on a problem or want to check over your work when you are using a calculator, consider the following questions.

- What is your estimate for the answer?
- How do you know your answer is correct?
- Does your answer make sense?
- Is this the only possible answer?

These directions are specific to the *Texas Instruments Math Explorer*. However, there are several other brands of fraction calculators such as *Casio,* that perform similar operations. Their instruction manuals will guide you through similar activities.

WARM UP
Turning On and Clearing—Using the (ON/AC), (CE/E), and (Backspace) Keys

(ON/AC)
- Look for the (ON/AC) key. When you press this key you should see a 0 in the display window. If you don't, press the (ON/AC) key once more to get 0. Most fraction calculators today are solar powered. Consequently, they do not have an OFF key. Return the calculator to its case when you are not using it.

- Press the (ON/AC) key twice; this clears all previous information that has been entered in the display and the memory. AC stands for All Clear.

(CE/E)
- Look for the (CE/E) key. Enter 43 + 5, push (CE/E), then 2 = . What happens? You should have a sum of 45, rather than 47. The (CE/E) key cleared the 5 and you replaced it with 2. The calculator added 43 + 2 when you entered = . The (CE/E) key clears the last entry when you push it once. When you push it twice it clears all numbers in the display, but not in the memory. To clear the memory you need to push (ON/AC).

(Backspace)
Enter 12345. Push (Backspace) once. What happens? Push (Backspace) again. What happens? Push (Backspace) two more times. What happens? The (Backspace) key deletes the last digit entered in the display.

Fraction Calculator Explorations

Basic Arithmetic

• The fraction calculator works just like the basic calculators you may have used before. Try at least one addition, subtraction, multiplication, and division problem.

$$123 + 45 \qquad 123 - 56 \qquad 123 \times 3 \qquad 123 \div 4$$

Probably the most fascinating aspect of these calculators is what they can do with fractions.

Calculating with Fractions—Using the ⬚/⬚ Key

• Find the ⬚/⬚ key. Enter
$$1 \; \fbox{/} \; 3 + 1 \; \fbox{/} \; 2 = .$$

What do you get? 5/6? The calculator adds fractions without you having to change them to decimals first!

Try, $1 \; \fbox{/} \; 3 + 1 \; \fbox{/} \; 4 = .$
Did you get 7/12?
What about $1 \; \fbox{/} \; 2 + 1 \; \fbox{/} \; 4 = ?$

Simplifying Fractions—Using N/D→n/d and the (Simp) Key

• Enter $1 \; \fbox{/} \; 6 + 14 \; \fbox{/} \; 24 = .$ Did you get 18/24?

Notice the N/D→n/d in the answer display on the left. This symbol tells you the fraction in the display can be simplified or reduced. (Remember, to reduce a fraction you divide the numerator and denominator by the same number—a factor of both.) You can choose the factor to divide by or you can let the calculator choose. Find the (Simp) key.

• If you want to choose the factor 6 for the above problem, enter
(Simp) 6 = . You get 3/4.

If you choose a number that is not a factor of both the numerator and the denominator, the calculator ignores you and 18/24 still shows with the N/D→n/d .

• To let the calculator choose the factor,

> Enter (Simp) = . With the first calculation you have $\frac{9}{12}$
> with N/D →n/d still showing.
> Enter (Simp) = again and you have $\frac{3}{4}$.

To check the factor that the calculator chose, push the (X⇄Y) key.
(To get back to your answer push (X⇄Y) again.)

• Experiment using the (Simp) key. Try a variety of problems.

Converting Decimals to Fractions and Vice Versa—
Using the (F⇄D) Key

• This key converts fractions to decimals and vice versa. Enter a
fraction and push the (F⇄D). Try a decimal and push the (F⇄D).
(*Note:* you might get a fraction that can be simplified.) See *The
Fraction, Decimal, Percent Connection* activity for more on the
relationships between fractions and decimals.

Mixed Numbers and Improper Fractions—
Using the (Unit) and (Ab/c) Keys

• On this calculator, you don't have to convert *mixed numbers* to
improper fractions to add them.

• Find the (Unit) key. To add the mixed numbers 2 $\frac{1}{3}$ + 4 $\frac{1}{6}$,

> Enter 2 (Unit) 1 (/) 3 + 4 (Unit) 1 (/) 6 = .
> You get 6 u $\frac{3}{6}$ with a N/D →n/d .
> Push (Simp) = to reduce and you have 6 u $\frac{1}{2}$ or 6 $\frac{1}{2}$.

• Suppose you start with two proper fractions:
> 7 (/) 8 + 4 (/) 5 = .

You get the improper fraction $\frac{67}{40}$. Find the (Ab/c) key. You can
change $\frac{67}{40}$ to a mixed number by pushing (Ab/c) and get 1 u $\frac{27}{40}$ or
1$\frac{27}{40}$. However, the calculator cannot change a mixed number to an
improper fraction.

• Experiment with some fraction problems using the (Unit) and
(Ab/c) keys.

Fraction Calculator Explorations

Percents—Using the ⬚%⬚ Key

• Find the ⬚%⬚ key. To calculate 12.5% of 400, enter 12.5 ⬚%⬚ . Stop and look at the display. What has happened? The calculator converted the percent to a decimal, just as you would with pencil and paper. Continue and enter x 400 = and you get 50.

• Try some other percent problems.

• The calculator can also find *percent decrease* and *percent increase*. Suppose you want to mark down a price of $80 by 20%,
> enter 80 − 20 ⬚%⬚ = .
> And you get 64, for a price of $64.

Notice that 16 showed in the display after you entered the ⬚%⬚. Why is that?

• To calculate a 30% increase in a price of $45, enter
> 45 + 30 ⬚%⬚ =.
> And you get 58.5 for a price of $58.50.

• Try some other percent problems using this key.

Constant Features—Using the ⬚Cons⬚ Key

• You can do repeated operations in two ways on the fraction calculator. When you use the ⬚Cons⬚ key (Cons stands for constant), the calculator keeps track of how many times you have done the operation. Both methods are slightly different than those for most basic four-function calculators. You may want to explore only one of the methods for each operation; or both and discuss the difference between what happens.

Repeated Addition

When you see three dots in a list of numbers or sequence of operations, they indicate that you continue indefinitely. For example, if you were counting by 10's, you would get 10, 20, 30... .You might say that the three dots stand for "and so on."

• The first way to skip count by 2's or find the multiples of 2 is to
> enter 2 + 2, followed by repeated = signs.
> You will get the sequence of numbers 2, 4, 6, 8,... .

• The second way is to use the ⬚Cons⬚ key. Find that button. To skip count by 2's, enter
> + 2 ⬚Cons⬚ , then 0, ⬚Cons⬚ , ⬚Cons⬚ , ...

What do you see in the display? Each time you push ⬚Cons⬚ a 2 is added on to the last number. Moreover, a counter runs on the left of the display that tells you how many times you have added 2 or what multiple of 2 you have.

Note: If you just enter + 2 (Cons), (Cons), (Cons), ... — without the 0 — the counter will tell you how many 2's have been added to 2, rather than what multiple of 2 you have reached.

• Set up the calculator to count by 7's, starting from 0. Find a number that surprises you. How many times does 7 divide that number?

• You can also experiment adding a constant starting with a different number. For example, enter
+ 4 (Cons) 27 (Cons), (Cons), and so on.

What's going on? You are adding 4 each time you enter (Cons) and the counter tells you how many times you have added 4 to 27. What happens when you enter
4 + 27 = = = =, and so on ?

Can you explain why you get a different sequence of answers?

• Try some other examples.

Repeated Subtraction
• For the first method, enter
30 – 2 = = = =, and so on.

What is happening? What happens eventually?

• For the second method, enter
– 2 (Cons), then 30 (Cons), (Cons), (Cons), and so on.

What happens? What does the counter on the left of the display tell you? The calculator subtracts 2 from the last number in the display each time you enter (Cons) and the counter tells you how many times you have subtracted 2. How many subtractions does it take to get to 0? What does this tell you about how many 2's are "in" 30?

• What happens when you get around 0 when you enter
– 8 (Cons) 100 (Cons), (Cons), (Cons), ... ?

Did you find that 12 subtractions gives you 4 and 13 subtractions gives you -4? What does this tell you about how many times 8 "goes into" 100?

• Try some other examples using the constant subtraction feature.

Fraction Calculator Explorations

Repeated Multiplication
• For the first method, enter
                2 x 2 = = = = = =, and so on.
What happens? Can you describe how you get the next number in the sequence? What happens eventually? When you see the "Error 0" display, did you really make a mistake or did the calculator just run out of space to store the number?

• For the second method, enter
                x 2 (Cons), then 1 (Cons), (Cons), (Cons),... .

What happens? You should have the same pattern that starts with 2 and continues to double to give 2, 4, 8, 16, 32, and so on. These are the powers of 2. The counter tells you what power of 2 you have gotten to. (What happens if you enter a different number than 1 in the above pattern?)

• Experiment finding powers of some other numbers.

Repeated Division
• For the first method, enter
                64 ÷ 2 = = =... .

What is happening? What happens after you get to 1? Can you write the decimal numbers you get as fractions? Is there a pattern?

• For the second method, enter
                ÷ 2 (Cons), then 64 and (Cons), (Cons), (Cons),... .
What happens?

You start with 64 and get half of the number in the display each time you enter (Cons). The counter tells you how many times you have divided by 2. How many divisions does it take to get to 1? What does this tell you? What happens next?

• What happens when you try this with 100 instead of 64?
                Enter ÷ 2 (Cons) 100 (Cons), (Cons), (Cons),... .

• What about
                ÷ 4 (Cons) 131,072 (Cons), (Cons), (Cons), and so on?

How did we know to start with 131,072?

• Explore some other examples using the divide constant feature.

Order of Operations—Using the ◁▢ and ▢▷ Keys

• Try the following arithmetic problems and compare your answers with your family:

$$27 - 5 \times 2 + 17,$$
$$4 \times 8 - 6 \times 2,$$
$$25 + 3 \times 3 - 2,$$
$$20 - 2 \times 10 + 8.$$

Did you all get the same answers; if not can you figure out why the answers were different?

• Now try the problems using the fraction calculator. Are you surprised? How is the calculator working out the problems? Look at $27 - 5 \times 2 + 17$. What do you get if you start with 27 subtract 5, then multiply by 2, and then add 17? Did you get 61? Does that agree with the calculator? What did the calculator do to get a different answer?

• What happens for $4 \times 8 - 6 \times 2$? If you start at the beginning and keep going, you get $32 - 6$ or 26×2, which equals 52. But the calculator gets 20? Why?

• Look at the last two problems. Can you explain why there are different answers. Do you know which answers are correct and why?

• Have you heard of the *order of operations?* Try the problems again using the fraction calculator. Notice that the calculator does not do any calculations until you press =. It waits to collect all of the input and then performs the arithmetic according to the rules for the order of operations. These rules are summarized in the sidebar.

When a problem contains a sequence of addition, subtraction, multiplication, and division operations, do the multiplication and division first and then do the addition and subtraction working from left to right, unless there are parentheses that guide you to do otherwise.

These rules are a convenient convention to assure that everyone is doing the problem the same way.

• Look at the first problem: $27 - 5 \times 2 + 17$. According to the rules, first we multiply 5×2 to get 10; then we have $27 - 10$ or 17. Finally we add 17. If you subtracted first, then multiplied by 2 and finally added 17 to get 61, your arithmetic wasn't wrong, but you were not following the rules for the order of operations. Most people would say the problem was wrong even though the arithmetic wasn't. In short, everyone follows the convention.

• Find the ◁▢ and ▢▷ keys. If you want to add or subtract before you multiply or divide in a problem, you need to use the parenthesis keys. For example, if you want to add $234 + 55$ and then multiply by 3, enter ◁▢ $234 + 55$ ▢▷ $\times$ 3.

• Make up some problems with parentheses that change the order of operations.

Do we have to learn rollerblading <u>and</u> middle school math at the same time?

Jobs that contribute to this world economy require workers who are mentally fit—workers who are prepared to absorb new ideas, to adapt to change, to cope with ambiguity. It is *these* needs, not just the need for calculation (which is now done mostly by machines), that make mathematics a prerequisite to so many jobs. More than ever before Americans need to think for a living; more than ever before, they need to think mathematically.

Everybody Counts, p.1.

Fraction Calculator Explorations

**Integer Division and Conversions—
Using the ⟮INT÷⟯ Key Division**
Find the integer division button, ⟮INT÷⟯ .

• Enter 34 ⟮INT÷⟯ 5 = . What happens? Look at the two sections of the screen, one with a Q and the second with a R. The first gives the whole number or *integer quotient* answer, to the division problem and the second the *remainder* (what is left over). In the problem above, you get a quotient of 6 with a remainder of 4.

• Try 3859 ⟮INT÷⟯ 6 =. Try some other division problems using integer divide.

Conversions
• Have you ever had to convert inches to feet, feet to yards, or minutes to hours? You can use the integer division button to help you. Suppose you want to convert 378 inches to feet.
Enter 378 ⟮INT÷⟯ 12 =.

What happens? You get 31 remainder 6 or 31 feet and 6 inches. What if you want to convert 49 feet to yards?
Enter 49 ⟮INT÷⟯ 3 =.

You get 16 (yards) and 1 (foot). Experiment with some other conversions.

Reciprocals—Using the ⟮1/x⟯ Key
Find the key marked ⟮1/x⟯ .

• Enter a 2. What happens when you push the ⟮1/x⟯ key next? What happens when you enter a 4 and then push the ⟮1/x⟯ key? What happens when you enter 5, push the ⟮1/x⟯ key and then push the ⟮1/x⟯ key a second time? Experiment with some other numbers. What does that key do to the number in the display?

• This key, ⟮1/x⟯ , is the *reciprocal key*. It divides 1 by the number in the display. The answer is called the *reciprocal* of the original number. Some people say two numbers are reciprocals if their product (the answer when you multiply them together) is one. Can you explain why?

• What happens when you enter a number and push the reciprocal key twice? Why?

Fixing a Decimal Point—Using the ⌜Fix⌟ Key
Rounding Numbers to a Fixed Number of Places
• Suppose you are doing some division problems and want everything rounded to only two decimal places. One problem might be 38492 ÷ 7. First try the division to see what you get.

Enter 38492 ÷ 7 = and you get 5498.8571.

Now find the ⌜Fix⌟ button.
Enter ⌜Fix⌟ 2. What happens?
Now enter 38492 ÷ 7 = . Do you get 5498.86?

Comparing Approximations of π
• Let's compare how good an approximation $^{22}\!/_7$ is for π to five decimal places. Find and push the π button; write out the number you get to five decimal places. (3.14159) (Do you need to round up for the last place?)
Enter ⌜Fix⌟ 5, 22 ÷ 7 = . Do you get 3.14286?

Pi, written as the symbol π, is the ratio of the circumference of a circle to its diameter. This number is always the same, no matter the size of the circle. The most common expression of this ratio is the formula for the circumference of a circle, C = πd or C = 2πr, where r stands for the radius of the circle.

Do you think this is close enough? Discuss this question with your group.

• Look up π in an encyclopedia or math book and be ready to report on your findings.

Changing Signs—Using the ⌜+⇄-⌟ Key
• Look for the key that is marked ⌜+⇄-⌟ . This key changes the sign of the number in the display from positive to negative or negative to positive. It is most useful when you want to perform operations with two or more negative numbers, especially when subtracting or multiplying two negative numbers. For example, if you need to calculate ⁻4 – ⁻9,
enter 4 ⌜+⇄-⌟ – 9 + ⌜+⇄-⌟ =.

Do you get 5? You can check the answer using a number line that has positive and negative numbers. You move right when you subtract a negative number.
• To calculate ⁻2 x ⁻8,
enter 2 ⌜+⇄-⌟ x 8 ⌜+⇄-⌟ =.

Do you get 16? Remember the old rule: "A minus times a minus is a plus?" What happens for 4 x ⁻4?
Enter 4 x 4 ⌜+⇄-⌟ =.

Did you get ⁻16? A positive times a negative is a negative.

Fraction Calculator Explorations

Powers and Exponents Using the $\boxed{x^2}$ Key

• When we multiply 2 by itself over and over again, mathematicians say that we are *finding powers of 2*. Here are the first six powers of 2.

first power	2^1	=	2	=	2
second power	2^2	=	2 x 2	=	4
third power	2^3	=	2 x 2 x 2	=	8
fourth power	2^4	=	2 x 2 x 2 x 2	=	16
fifth power	2^5	=	2 x 2 x 2 x 2 x 2	=	32
sixth power	2^6	=	2 x 2 x 2 x 2 x 2 x 2	=	64

The small raised number to the right of the 2's is called an *exponent*. It denotes how many 2's are multiplied to get that power. The exponents match the powers.

• When we calculate 2 x 2, we say we are *finding the square of 2* or *raising 2 to the second power*. In the problem 2 x 2 x 2, we say we are *finding the cube of 2*, or *finding the third power of 2*. When we calculate 2^4, we say that we are *raising 2 to the fourth power*.

• Look for the $\boxed{x^2}$ key. Enter 3 and push the $\boxed{x^2}$ key. What happens? Try some other numbers. Do you know what this key does? It calculates the square of the number.
Enter 36 + 7 $\boxed{x^2}$.

• What do you think the answer will be? What do you get when you push =? Are you surprised? What does this have to do with the order of operations?

• What happens when you enter
2 $\boxed{x^2}$, $\boxed{x^2}$, $\boxed{x^2}$, . . . ?

Using the $\boxed{10^n}$ Key

• Find the $\boxed{10^n}$ key. Enter $\boxed{10^n}$ 3. What happens?

Try some other numbers with the $\boxed{10^n}$ key. What does that key do? What happens for these entries:
21.4 x $\boxed{10^n}$ 3 =; .0523 x $\boxed{10^n}$ 4 =; 27.85 x $\boxed{10^n}$ 3 =?

Is there a faster way to do these problems?

Using the $\boxed{y^x}$ Key

• Find the $\boxed{y^x}$ key. Enter 2 $\boxed{y^x}$ 6 = . What do you get? What happened? You calculated 2^6 or 2 x 2 x 2 x 2 x 2 x 2.

• Try the following problems and explain what happens. Be sure to clear the calculator after each problem.

$$3 \ \boxed{y^x} \ 4 =$$
$$2 \ \boxed{y^x} \ 4 =$$
$$14 \ \boxed{y^x} \ 3 =$$
$$4 \ \boxed{y^x} \ 3 =$$

• Make up some problems for your family.

Roots
Square Roots—Using the $\boxed{\sqrt{}}$ Key

• Find the $\boxed{\sqrt{}}$ key. What happens when you enter 81 followed by $\boxed{\sqrt{}}$? What about 49 $\boxed{\sqrt{}}$?

For example, $\sqrt{81} = 9$, because 9 x 9 = 81; $\sqrt{49} = 7$, because 7 x 7 = 49. Note, we write $\sqrt{81}$, but need to enter 81 $\boxed{\sqrt{}}$ on the calculator to get the square root of 81.

The $\sqrt{}$ on the key is a *square root* or *radical sign*. When you take a square root of a number, you find the number that produces the original number when it is squared.

• What happens when you enter 2 $\boxed{\sqrt{}}$? You get 1.4142136 or $\sqrt{2}$ to seven places. If you enter x^2 next, you get 2. But if you multiply 1.4142136 x 1.4142136, you get 2.0000001. Do you know why this happens?

Some numbers have square roots that are *irrational*. They are numbers with never-ending decimals. The square root of 2 is irrational; 1.4142136 is just what fits in the display. This calculator is programmed so that if you square using the $\boxed{x^2}$ key, it rounds to two, but this does not happen when you square 1.4142136 by multiplying it by itself.

• The square roots of 2, 3, and 5 are irrational. Can you think of other irrational numbers?

Some numbers can be written as the ratio of two whole numbers. These are called *rational numbers*. Numbers that cannot be written as the ratio of two whole numbers are called *irrational numbers*.

Fraction Calculator Explorations

Other Roots

• Suppose you want to find a *cube root* of a number — the number n that when multiplied by itself three times, n x n x n, gives the original number. For example to calculate $\sqrt[3]{64}$,

enter 64 $\boxed{y^x}$ 1/3 = .

Did you get 4? To find the fifth root of 243 or $\sqrt[5]{243}$ — the number n which when multiplied by itself 5 times, n x n x n x n x n, gives 243,

enter 243 $\boxed{y^x}$ 1/5 = .

Did you get 3?

When you enter the ⅓ to find the cube root, you are entering an exponent of ⅓. Finding the cube root of a number is the same as finding the ⅓ power of that number. Finding the fifth root of a number is the same thing as finding the ⅕ power of that number, and so on.

• These problems tell us something interesting about roots and powers.

• Try some other problems involving roots.

Memory

• The memory keys help you keep track of a series of computations. Try finding the total expenses for a party. Suppose your class is having a party next week. You need to pick the food and estimate the costs in order to decide how much to charge each person. Suppose you want to buy the following:

7 liters of soda	@	$0.69 each
9 pizzas	@	$8.47 each
3 loaves garlic bread	@	$1.89 each
2 cakes	@	$5.49 each

• First quickly estimate how much you think you will spend.

• Now clear your calculator by pushing $\boxed{\text{ON/AC}}$ twice. Make sure that no M shows.

Find the $\boxed{M+}$, $\boxed{M-}$, and $\boxed{MR}$ keys.

Enter 7 x .69 =   *(you should have 4.83).*

Enter $\boxed{M+}$ *(you should see a small M on the left side of the display and 4.83 on the right).*

Enter 9 x 8.47 =   *(you should have 76.23 and an M).*

Enter **only once** $\boxed{M+}$

(there will be a blink, you will still see the M and 76.23).

If you push (M+) more than once, it will add the 76.23 to the memory each time you push (M+), giving you too high a total. To double check that the $76.23 really went into the memory,

enter (M R)	*(you should see 81.06; if you don't, start over).*
Enter 3 x 1.89 =	*(you should see 5.67 and an M).*
Enter (M+)	*(there will be a blink; you will see the M and 5.67).*
Enter 2 x 5.49 =	*(you will see 10.98 and M).*
Enter (M+), and	*(there will be a blink; you will see the M and 10.98).*
Enter (M R)	*(you should have a grand total of $97.71).*

How close was your estimate?

• Make up your own food list for a party with your table group. Assume you have a budget of $200, and you have to buy cups, plates, napkins, and forks. Don't forget to include the tax. Use the memory keys to calculate your costs.

Note: If you accidentally add a number, for example 5.51 to the memory, you can remove it. To do so,

enter 5.51 (M−)
to subtract 5.51 from the memory total. ∎

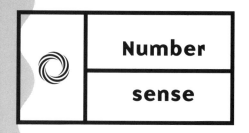

Resolving an Argument

MATERIALS

pencil and paper

blocks or beans

WHAT'S THE MATH?

Proportional reasoning; fractions.

How

• The following argument was reported on a radio newscast. Can you help out?

Sasha and Josephine are college friends who decide to share an apartment. Sasha was lucky enough to find a very good job right out of school, but Josephine is still looking for a permanent teaching job and only has occasional substituting jobs.

They decide they should split their expenses proportionally until Josephine gets full-time work. Sasha says since she is earning three times as much as Josephine right now, Josephine should pay one fourth of the expenses. Josephine says "Hey, I was going to pay one third of the expenses!"

• Work with a family member to decide who is right and why. Use diagrams, concrete objects such as blocks or beans, or charts to help you. Consider drawing a picture that shows the salaries and their relationship to each other.

• Be ready to share your reasoning with other groups. ■

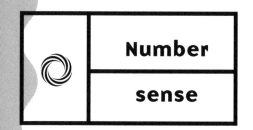

Resolving Another Argument

WHAT'S THE MATH?

Order of operations; the distributive property of multiplication over addition.

How

• Can you help resolve the following argument?

Steve and Henry volunteered to do the accounts for the school club. Several students worked during the month. Each student earns $6.27 an hour.

Steve complains to Henry that he has to do a lot of hard arithmetic to figure out how much the club has to pay in total salaries. He says he will have to multiply each person's hours by $6.27 and find the total.

Henry says, no, you can add up all the hours and then multiply that number by $6.27 to get the total.

Steve says that won't work?

Here are the hours.

Sarah	34.5
Hank	37.25
Manny	21.0
MaryJean	42.5
Greg	25.25
Bobbi Jo	32.0
Gloria	41.5

• What do you think? Why?

• Work with a family member to decide who is right and why. Use diagrams, concrete objects such as blocks, beans, or charts to help you.

• Be ready to share your reasoning with other groups. ■

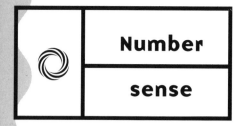

Number sense

Resolving a Third Argument

Understanding how percents work is important for everyday living. They help you figure out the best "deal" and to see if sales claims are misleading.

How

• Can you help to resolve the following arguments? Work with a family member to decide who is right and why. Use diagrams, concrete objects such as blocks or beans, or charts to help you.

Jesse and Mary are going to a sale.

First they stop at the shoe department. Shoes that were marked down 50% have an extra 30% off today. Jesse says, "Wow! That means the shoes are only 20% of the original price."

Mary disagrees. She says the shoes are 65% off the original price.

• Whom do you agree with? Why?

 Next Jesse and Mary go to buy some CDs. The CDs were marked down to 75% of the original price and you can take 30% more off today.

• Can you help Jesse and Mary figure out how much they will save on CDs before they get into another argument?

• Get ready to share your reasoning about both arguments with other groups. ■

Extension

• Look in newspapers and magazines or listen to radio and television to find a story that has a potential argument in it. Bring it to share.

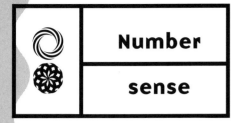

Calculating Patterns:
Looking at Multiples

In this activity calculators help to generate lists of multiples of numbers quickly. We'll look for patterns to help us recognize multiples of numbers.

The *multiples* of a number are all numbers that the original number divides evenly. A *factor* of a number is a whole number that divides it evenly.

How

• Make sure you have a calculator that has a feature that allows for repeated addition automatically. Many basic calculators work as follows. For counting by 2's, enter: 2 + 2 = = = =. Some have a special button for repeated or constant addition. Check your instruction booklet for further details.

• For each number listed below, use the constant addition feature on a calculator to skip count by the number and record the numbers you "land" on. For example, 2, 4, 6, 8, 10, and so on, is what you get when you skip count by 2's. These are *multiples of 2*. They all can be divided evenly by 2; that is, they are *divisible by 2*.

• Work in pairs. One person uses the calculator and the other records the numbers in a list.

• Count until you have passed 50 or 100.

• Study the list of multiples you have made. Look for patterns.

• Do the patterns help you know when a number is a multiple of the number you started with or can be divided by the starting number?

```
2
4
6
.
.
.
```

• Do you know how to recognize multiples of 2?
Discuss your ideas with your family.

• Work in pairs. Skip count by 2's. Record the results in a list. Go until you reach 50 or more.

• Study the list. What patterns do you see in the last or units place of the numbers? What does this tell you about the numbers that are multiples of 2 — the numbers that are divisible by 2? Will this work for numbers that are larger than those on your list? Why or why not?

• If you continue forever, would you hit every number that is divisible by 2? That is, will every number that is divisible by 2 be on the list? Why or why not?

• What can you say about numbers that are multiples of 5?

• Discuss your ideas and then work with a partner and the calculator to check the pattern in the multiples of 5.

• What can you say about recognizing multiples of 5? Will this work in all cases?

• What can you say about numbers that are multiples of 10?

Calculating Patterns:
Looking at Multiples

• Work with a partner and use the calculator to create a list of multiples of 3 that goes over 100.

• Study the list. Do you see any patterns in the units place? In the tens column? What about when you add up or sum the individual digits in each multiple?

• Discuss your ideas with your family.

• What can you say about numbers that are multiples of 3 — are divisible by 3? Be ready to share with other groups.

• Work with a partner and use the calculator to create a list of multiples of 4 that goes over 100.

• Study the list. Do you see any patterns in the units place? In the tens column? When you look at the last two digits together?

• Discuss your ideas with your family. What can you say about numbers that are multiples of 4 — are divisible by 4? Be ready to share with other groups.

• Work with a partner and use the calculator to create a list of multiples of 9 that goes over 100.

• Study the list. Do you see any patterns in the units place? In the tens column? When you add the digits of individual multiples? For example, for 27: 2 + 7 = 9.

• Discuss your ideas with your family. What can you say about numbers that are multiples of 9 — divisible by 9? Be ready to share with other groups.

• Work with a partner and use the calculator to create a list of multiples of 6 that goes over 100.

• Study the list. Do you see any patterns in the units place? In the tens column? When you sum the digits?

• Discuss your ideas with your family. What can you say about numbers that are multiples of 6 — are divisible by 6? Be ready to share with other groups.

• Work with a partner and use the calculator to create a list of multiples of 7 that goes over 100.

• Study the list. Do you see any patterns? Discuss your ideas with your family. What can you say about numbers that are multiples of 7 — are divisible by 7? Be ready to share with other groups.

Leader Notes

• If the students are familiar with divisibility patterns for 2, 5, and 10, skip directly to patterns for 3, and so on.

• Consider working on only one or two numbers in a class. ∎

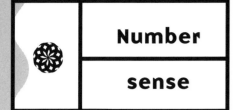
Exploring Divisibility Rules

You may remember rules about division, such as a number is divisible by 9 if the sum of its individual digits is divisible by nine. This activity uses the results from the *Calculating Patterns* activity and some other math ideas to explore why some of these rules work.

If a larger whole number can be divided by a smaller one leaving no remainder, we say the larger number is *divisible by* the smaller number. The larger number is called a *multiple* of the smaller one.

MATERIALS

pencil and paper

calculators

results from *Calculating Patterns* activity

WHAT'S THE MATH?

Multiples; patterns; divisibility; distributive property; expanded notation.

How

• Before we look at particular divisibility rules, there are some ideas about division to think about.

Statement I: If two numbers are each divisible by a smaller number, their sum is also divisible by that smaller number.

• This statement may sound confusing until we try some specific numbers. (Use pencil and paper or a calculator with an integer divide key that gives division answers with remainders, rather than decimals.) Let's say the two numbers are 27 and 30. Both are divisible by 3. What is their sum? (57) Is that divisible by 3? (Yes, 57 ÷ 3 = 19.)

• Do you get the same number if you divide first and then add? For example, for 27 and 30, does (27 ÷ 3) + (30 ÷ 3) = (27 + 30) ÷ 3?

• Try some more numbers that are divisible by 3. Try numbers that are divisible by 7, 4, 9, 5, or any others you want to test. Try enough numbers until you feel convinced that *Statement I* is true.

Statement II: If you multiply any number by a number that is divisible by a smaller number, the product is also divisible by the smaller number.

• Again, try some numbers to see if the statement works. Suppose you multiply 88 by 15. Since 15 is divisible by 3 and 5, then the product of 88 x 15 should also be divisible by 3 and 5. Check it out. Is the product also divisible by 2, 4, 8, and 11?

• Try other numbers. Can you explain why this works?

• We also need to look at the following situation. Suppose you have a number and one of its multiples, for example 3 and 9.
Is it true that if a number is divisible by 9, it is also divisible by 3?

Is it also true if a number is divisible by 3, that it is divisible by 9?

Discuss these questions with your family. Try some other numbers, such as 2 and 4, 3 and 6, or others of your choice. Be ready to share your thoughts.

Statement I is a way to state one of the properties about numbers, the Distributive Property of Division over Addition. *When dividing the sum of two numbers by a third number, we can add the two numbers and then divide, or divide the two numbers separately and then add.*

Exploring Divisibility Rules

• We will also use what is called expanded notation of numbers. This is the way to write numbers as a sum of units, tens, hundreds, thousands, and so on.

For example, the expanded form of 45,068 is

   4 ten thousands + 5 thousands + 0 hundreds + 6 tens + 8 units
or
   4 x 10,000 + 5 x 1,000 + 0 x 100 + 6 x 10 + 8
or
   $4 \times 10^4 + 5 \times 10^3 + 0 \times 10^2 + 6 \times 10 + 8$.

• Several divisibility rules or tests follow. We will use the explorations from above and results from *Calculating Patterns* to look at what makes them work.

A number is divisible by 3 if the sum of its individual digits is divisible by 3.

• Look at your notes about the sums of the digits of multiples of three from *Calculating Patterns* and try some larger numbers to see if the rule still holds. You can use a calculator with integer division to help you find large numbers to test. Do you think the rule works for all numbers that are multiples of 3?

• To explain why the rule works, we will use expanded notation and *Statement I*. Look at a large number such as 56,871.

Write it in expanded form:
   5 x 10,000 + 6 x 1,000 + 8 x 100 + 7 x 10 + 1.

Look at the following:
   10,000 = 9,999 + 1; 1,000 = 999 + 1; 100 = 99 + 1; and 10 = 9 + 1.

Replacing the powers of tens with these new numbers, 56,871 can be written as:

5 x (9,999 + 1) + 6 x (999 +1) + 8 x (99 + 1) + 7 x (9 +1) +1,

which is the same as

5 x 9,999 + 5 + 6 x 999 + 6 + 8 x 99 + 8 + 7 x 9 + 7 + 1.

or

5 x 9,999 + 6 x 999 + 8 x 99 + 7 x 9 + 5 + 6 + 8 + 7+ 1.

We know that 9,999; 999; 99; and 9 are all divisible by 3, so all of the numbers under the bracket are divisible by 3. They are added to 5 + 6 + 8 + 7 + 1 = 27, which is also divisible by 3. But if two numbers that are divisible by 3 are added, their sum is also divisible by 3, so 56,871 is divisible by 3.

No matter what numbers are under the bracket, we will always have a total that is divisible by 3. What is left over is just the sum of the digits of the number. If those are divisible by 3, the entire number is also divisible by 3.

• Experiment with some more large numbers. Use the rule for divisibility by 3 and check with pencil and paper or calculator. If you use a calculator with integer division, compare the remainder on the calculator to the remainder when dividing the sum of the digits by 3.

*A number is divisible by 6 if it is divisible by 3 **and by** 2, if it is even and the sum of its digits is divisible by 3.*

• We know numbers that are divisible by 2 are even. And we know how to tell if a number is divisible by 3.

• Why do numbers that are divisible by 6 have to be divisible by both 2 and 3? Discuss this question with your family. *Hint:* Compare the list of multiples of 2, 3, and 6. Remember that any number that is divisible by 6 can be written as 6 (or 3 x 2) times another number; for example

666 = 6 x 111 = 3 x 2 x 111;

5,490 = 6 x 915 = 3 x 2 x 915;

96 = 6 x 16 = 3 x 2 x 16.

Exploring Divisibility Rules

A number is divisible by 9 if the sum of its individual digits is divisible by 9.

• Look at 56,879. Write it in expanded form as we did in the section on 3. What can you say about the numbers that include 9,999; 999; 99; and 9? What's left? Why is 56,879 divisible by 9?

• Discuss why these ideas work for all numbers that are multiples of 9. Use a calculator with integer division and try some large numbers. Compare the remainders when you divide by 9 to those when the sum of the digits is divided by 9.

A number is divisible by 4 if the last 2 digits are divisible by 4.

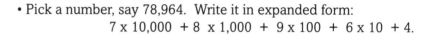

• Pick a number, say 78,964. Write it in expanded form:
$$7 \times 10{,}000 + 8 \times 1{,}000 + 9 \times 100 + 6 \times 10 + 4.$$

Check that 10,000; 1,000; and 100 are divisible by 4. (What about 100,000, 1,000,000, 10,000,000, and so on?) This means the number is divisible by 4 if
$$6 \times 10 + 4 = 64 \text{ is divisible by 4.}$$

No matter what digits multiply the 10,000, 1,000, and 100, their products will be divisible by 4. So a number is divisible by 4 if the last two digits are divisible by 4.

• Try some large numbers to test the rule. Use a calculator with integer division to compare the remainders when you divide by 4 to those when you divide the last two digits by 4.

A number is divisible by 8 if the last three digits are divisible by 8.

• Look at 1,000; 10,000; 100,000; 1,000,000. Are they divisible by 8? What about larger powers of 10 such as 10,000,000, 100,000,000, and so on?

• Try 867,888. Use the example for 4's as a model. Write out 867,888 in expanded notation and show that divisibility by 8 depends on the divisibility of the last three digits. Why is it necessary to look at the last three digits this time rather than just the last two?

• Try some large numbers to test the rule. Use a calculator with integer division to compare the remainders when you divide by 8 to those when you divide the last three digits by 8.

There are some rules for divisibility by 7 and 11, but they are more complicated to carry out than the ones we have seen, and much more difficult to explain.

Leader Notes

• You may want to set up the first explorations as Openers and then discuss the results when you begin this activity with the group as a whole. ■

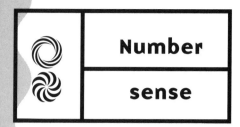
The Game of 15

How

MATERIALS
number strips
two colors of markers

WHAT'S THE MATH?
Mental arithmetic and
logical thinking.

• You will need a partner, one number strip, and 7 or 8 markers each.

• Choose a marker color.

• Take turns placing a marker on the number strip.

• The object is to be the first one who has three markers to cover numbers that add to 15.

• Play several times. Then, discuss the best approach to the game. See if you can work out a winning strategy with your partner. Share your ideas with another pair.

Variations
• Play with a longer strip, using a higher target number with four or five markers.

• Use two colors of markers, for each player. Suppose you chose red and blue. Place a red marker on numbers to add to your total and a blue marker on those you want to subtract.

• Work with a partner to see if you can obtain a target number using addition and subtraction covering all the numbers on a strip. ■

| 1 | 2 | 3 | 4 | 5 | 6 | 7 | 8 | 9 |

Nonconsecutive Number Boxes

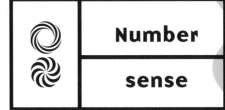

This activity shows how using manipulatives contributes to problem solving.

Consecutive numbers follow each other when you count.

How

• Work with a partner.

• Arrange the numbers 1, 2, 3, 4, 5, 6, 7, 8 in grid A, so no two consecutive numbers are in squares with a common side or corner (vertex).

• Do the same for grid B.

• Use 1 through 10 for grid C and follow the same rules.

• Do you think your solutions are unique?

MATERIALS
number grids

numbers squares 0 through 10

WHAT'S THE MATH?
Spatial and logical reasoning.

Extensions

• Experiment with different grids to make up your own puzzle. Double check that there is a solution and give it to a friend to solve.

• Discuss what kinds of grids work for these types of puzzles. Are there any that would be impossible?

A

B

C

| 1 | 2 | 3 | 4 | 5 | 6 | 7 | 8 | 9 | 10 |

Exploring Number Sequences

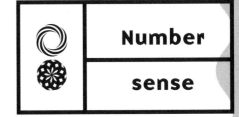

Number sense

The idea of investigating number sequences to strengthen number sense, reinforce algebraic thinking, and introduce more advanced concepts comes from an Oregon high school teacher. Many of the questions he raises are very relevant to middle school mathematics.

Preparation
Write out each sequence on adding machine tape or butcher paper. Use the colors indicated. Be sure the numbers are large and dark enough to be read at a distance. Post the four sequences in class so that all families will be able to see them. Make copies of the Sequence Chart for each participant to use.

Purple: 2; 3; 5; 7; 11; 13; 17; 19; 23; 29; 31; 37; 41; 43; 47; 53; 59; 61; 67; 71; 73; 79; 83; 89; 97

Blue: 2; 4; 8; 16; 32; 64; 128; 256; 512; 1,024; 2,048; 4,096; 8,192; 16,384; 32,768; 65,536; 131,072; 262,144; 524,288; 1,048,576

Green: 1; 8; 27; 64; 125; 216; 343; 512; 729, 1,000; 1,331; 1,728; 2,197; 2,744; 3,375; 4,096; 4,913; 5,832; 6,859; 8,000

Red: 1; 4; 9; 16; 25; 36; 49; 64; 81; 100; 121; 144; 169; 196; 225; 256; 289; 324; 361; 400; 441; 484; 529; 576; 625; 676; 729; 784; 841; 900

MATERIALS
pencil and paper

calculators

number sequences on
   butcher paper or
   adding machine tape

WHAT'S THE MATH?
Prime numbers; squares; cubes; powers of 2; twin primes; properties of exponents; Pythagorean triples; Fermat's Last Theorem; comparing patterns.

This activity is based on an article by Don Crossfield in the February 1997 *Math Teacher.*

Exploring Number Sequences

How

• Use the number sequences to explore the questions below. Work with your family and table group. Be ready to share what you have found with other groups. You can use notes, tables, and diagrams to describe your work.

Finding Numbers and Terms in the Sequences

• What number comes next in each sequence? How did you figure this out? What is the rule that generates each sequence? What is the rule that tells you each *term* (number) *in the sequence?* Does numbering the terms help you with this question?

Sums of Terms

• When you add two numbers, the answer is called the sum. Find two numbers in the same color that have a sum that is the same color. Can you do this on all of the lists? Can you find more than one example on each list?

The purple sequence is prime numbers; *the blue,* powers of 2; *the green,* cubes; *and the red,* squares.

Purple pairs of the form (p, p + 2), for example (11, 13) and (29, 31), are called twin primes. *There may be an infinite number of these pairs; however, no one has proved this yet.*

When the sum (c) of two red numbers (a and b) is also in the red sequence, these numbers are called a Pythagorean triple. *For all of these triples, you will find $a^2 + b^2 = c^2$. It is also possible to draw a right triangle with sides of length a, b, and c for each of these triples.*

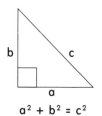

$$a^2 + b^2 = c^2$$

The fact that we can't find any pairs of numbers with their sum in the green sequence is related to Fermat's Last Theorem, *that states we cannot find whole numbers or fractions for which $a^n + b^n = c^n$ when n is greater than 2. In 1637, Fermat noted this theorem in the margins of a Greek math book from the third century. He claimed he had found remarkable proof for the theorem, which the margin was too narrow to contain. Even though many mathematicians have worked on this problem, it was not proved until 1993 by Andrew Wiles. He had been fascinated with the problem since he was 10 years old and put aside all other research for seven years to complete the proof. His work built on the ideas and theorems of many contemporary mathematicians.*

Products of Terms

• When you multiply two numbers together the answer is called the *product;* the two numbers are *factors* of that product.

• Find two numbers of the same color that have a product that is the same color. Can you find more than one example? Can you find examples on all of the lists? What happens when you square a blue number? A green number? A red number?

A prime number has only one and itself as factors. Consequently, we will not be able to find two numbers and their product on the purple list.

The product of any pair of numbers on the blue list is on the blue list. This is related to the rules for exponents and the relationships between powers of 2. What about pairs of numbers on the green list?

Doubles

• Can you find a number whose double is the same color? On which lists? Can you explain why?

This won't work on the purple prime number list. The reasons are related to what happens when you double odd numbers and the definition of prime numbers.

You also cannot find doubles on the list of cubes or squares. Neither the square root of 2 nor the square root of 3 can be written as a whole number or fraction.

Common Numbers

• How many blue numbers are on the red list? What fraction of red numbers are on the blue list? Are these fractions the same? Why do you think this happens?

Looking at patterns of the exponents in these sequences helps explain when and how a number from one list can belong to the other.

Digit Patterns

What patterns can you find in the one's place of each list?

Leader Notes

• Consider using the number sequences throughout the whole FAMILY MATH series. Have the families explore one or two of the questions in each class. ■

Exploring Number Sequences

Position	Purple	Blue	Green	Red
1	2	2	1	1
2	3	4	8	4
3	5	8	27	9
4	7	16	64	16
5	11	32	125	25
6	13	64	216	36
7	17	128	343	49
8	19	256	512	64
9	23	512	729	81
10	29	1,024	1,000	100
11	31	2,048	1,331	121
12	37	4,096	1,728	144
13	41	8,192	2,197	169
14	43	16,384	2,744	196
15	47	32,768	3,375	225
16	53	65,536	4,096	256
17	59	131,072	4,913	289
18	61	262,144	5,832	324
19	67	524,288	6,859	361
20	71	1,048,576	8,000	400
21	73	2,097,152	9,261	441
22	79	4,194,304	10,648	484
23	83	8,388,608	12,167	529
24	89	16,777,216	13,824	576
25	97	33,554,432	15,625	625
26	101	67,108,864	17,576	676
27	103	134,217,728	19,683	729
28	107	268,435,456	21,952	784
29	109	536,870,912	24,389	841
30	113	1,073,741,824	27,000	900

Postage Problem

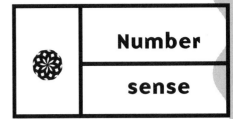

Has anyone in your family asked you to find the exact postage for, say, $1.17 on an envelope, when you had a pile of 32¢ stamps and several 19¢ stamps and a couple of 3¢ stamps? You have to figure out the best combination of stamps to use. Often you have to decide whether to overpay by a few cents or take the time to go to the post office to get stamps for the exact amount. This activity presents a similar situation.

You are visiting a country that has only 5¢ and 8¢ stamps. The postmaster wants to know what postage rates can be charged using just these types of stamps. She would like you to check out all of the postage values from 1¢ to 99¢.

How

• Do you think you can charge postage from 1¢ to 99¢, using only 5¢ and 8¢ stamps? Work in your family groups to find some of the values you can charge. Do you think there are some that won't work?

• Discuss with your group the best way to tackle the task of checking all the values from 1¢ to 99¢. Divide up the work.

• Make a record of your work to share with other groups. As you work, discuss what types of mathematics you are using. Look for patterns. Be ready to share your information with other groups.

• Study your results to see if you can find a number beyond which all numbers "work." Mathematicians call that number the *conductor* of 5 and 8.

MATERIALS

scratch paper and pencils

paper square "stamps"

calculators

hundreds chart (p. 252)

WHAT'S THE MATH?

Multiples; mental arithmetic; recording information; logical thinking.

Postage Problem

Our colleague Steve Jordan from University of Illinois at Chicago said this activity is a particular case of a more general mathematics problem from number theory. Ferdinand Georg Frobenius (1849–1917) found a rule for finding the conductor of two numbers that have no common factors other than one. Multiply one less than the first number by one less than the second. In our example that would mean the conductor is 4 x 7 or 28. Is that what you found? Frobenius also proved that the number of gaps, or numbers you can't find, is equal to half of the conductor. Does that work for our example?

Extension

- Investigate postage values for other pairs of stamps such as 5¢ and 2¢; 5¢ and 13¢; 5¢ and 4¢; 5¢ and 10¢; or any other pair that interests you. Can you make any predictions about the outcomes before you start?

8¢	8¢	8¢	8¢	8¢	8¢	8¢
8¢	8¢	8¢	8¢	8¢	8¢	8¢
8¢	8¢	8¢	8¢	8¢	8¢	8¢
8¢	8¢	8¢	8¢	8¢	8¢	8¢
8¢	8¢	8¢	8¢	8¢	8¢	8¢
8¢	8¢	8¢	8¢	8¢	8¢	8¢
8¢	8¢	8¢	8¢	8¢	8¢	8¢
5¢	5¢	5¢	5¢	5¢	5¢	5¢
5¢	5¢	5¢	5¢	5¢	5¢	5¢
5¢	5¢	5¢	5¢	5¢	5¢	5¢
5¢	5¢	5¢	5¢	5¢	5¢	5¢

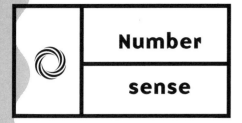

Value of Words Revisited

This activity is an extension to the *Value of Words* activity in the original *FAMILY MATH* book.

This activity provides experiences examining a series of cases for a mathematical question. The kind of thinking involved is important in algebra and geometry, as well as many other advanced mathematics courses.

CHEAP WORDS

PRICEY WORDS

DICTIONARY

MATERIALS

pencil and paper

calculators

WHAT'S THE MATH?

Mental arithmetic;
estimation; logical thinking.

How

• Assign values to letters as shown.

A = $1	J = $10	S = $19
B = $2	K = $11	T = $20
C = $3	L = $12	U = $21
D = $4	M = $13	V = $22
E = $5	N = $14	W = $23
F = $6	O = $15	X = $24
G = $7	P = $16	Y = $25
H = $8	Q = $17	Z = $26
I = $9	R = $18	

• Work with your family to see how many words you can find with values from $1 to $100. Keep a record of your work to share with others.

• Are there any values between $1 and $100 you think will be impossible to find words for? If this is so, can you explain why? Might your answer be different for a language other than English?

• Collect words from the whole group to see how many different words you have found for each value.

• Can you find a sentence worth $1,000? $1,500? $2,000? ■

Extensions

• Find values for words from languages other than English. Some languages such as Hawaiian and Finnish have more vowels and longer words than English. Some, such as Polish or Welsh, have more consonants. How do you think these conditions will affect the value of common words in Hawaiian, Finnish, Polish, and Welsh? Look in the library for dictionaries to help answer this question.

Statistics Extension

• Work on this activity two or three times. Then, collect all of the words. Use a graph to examine and determine information such as most frequent letter, least frequent vowel, etc., in the word collection. Discuss the results with your family.

Parent Advocacy

Tools

The middle school years are critical for students both developmentally and academically. Children are beginning the transition from childhood to adulthood. At this age they are struggling with autonomy and want to make decisions about their own lives. Some adolescents are ready to handle the cause-and-effect nature of decision-making. However, the stakes are too high for educational decision-making to be left exclusively to them. Most middle school students do not fully understand how academic decisions will expand or limit future college and career options.

Parents face a multitude of pressing academic issues during these years. Particularly problematic are the areas of math and science. Schools provide some information for parents, but course information is not always easily understood. Many adults had negative experiences in math and are not able to be as much of a resource for their child as they would like. Additionally, if English is your second language or if your family is new to the community, seeking math and science resources may seem daunting.

Being an advocate for your child may require courage and persistence. However, parental involvement is key to supporting the course decision process. Your encouragement can make the decisive difference in the confidence, competence, and success your child experiences.

Understanding the components that will affect your child's mathematics success enables you to be active and informed. You can then become a partner to your child's mathematics achievement and help make the best course decisions.

We at FAMILY MATH believe that all children can learn and be successful in mathematics. The information in this section provides adults with tools to guide their child's mathematics education through the middle school grades, into high school, and on to college toward numerous career possibilities. Topics include the optimum time to take algebra, how you can help with math homework, math content covered in middle school, and the relationship between mathematics and high paying careers.

Can we escape into a time tunnel until they're 30 and self-supporting?

The African proverb, *"It takes a village to raise a child,"* is true. Extended family and friends can help you advocate for your child's educational and developmental interests. Grandparents, aunts, uncles, older siblings, and friends can be of assistance by investing time to ensure that children do not get lost in the educational maze. Meeting with teachers and school counselors, talking with other middle and high school parents, and attending school events will make your family more visible and promote the best interests of your child. ∎

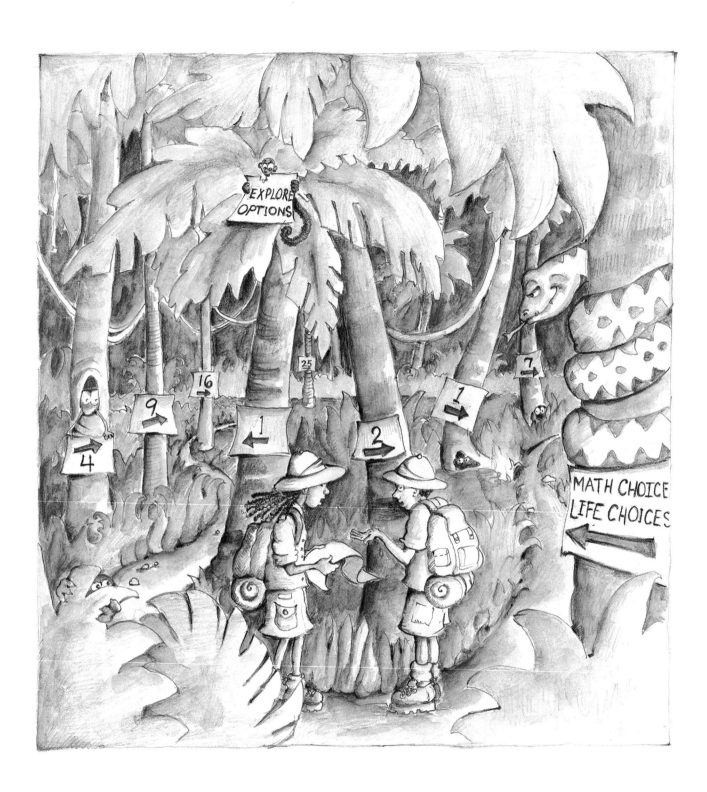

Tracking

Our Children

Schools serve many functions within our society, the primary one being to socialize our children. Parents send their children to school to get the tools, strategies, and information necessary to succeed as adults in society. Mathematics is one of the measures that determines how well a child is prepared.

Schools, like other institutions, need an efficient and productive way to deliver their services. The system most widely used in American schools is one where students are channeled or "tracked" into specific courses based on their perceived abilities or academic potential. The educational community constantly debates if or how tracking or ability grouping should be used. Everyone agrees that many of the outcomes do not meet the educational goals of society. Looking back at the history of tracking in America provides a context to understand these issues today.

Tracking—its beginning

Tracking or ability grouping dates back to the 18th century. It was devised to address diversity. Families from poor rural areas of the country, as well as immigrants from eastern and southern Europe, radically changed the student population. Separating students into groups based on perceived potential seemed to be an efficient method to integrate new students into the educational system. Tracking reflected societal beliefs that those citizens who were either poor or ethnically or racially different from the dominant culture were intellectually limited.

EQUALS and FAMILY MATH believe all children can succeed in mathematics. Tracking in mathematics restricts academic potential and consequently is harmful to children and society. We believe all children have the right to interesting and challenging curriculum. If the advanced math courses at your child's school do not reflect the school's diversity in gender and ethnicity, restrictive attitudes about which children receive opportunities may be present.

How is tracking used in schools today?

• While students in elementary school are certainly grouped by ability for many subjects, formal tracking truly begins at the middle school level. The difficulty and complexity of middle school curriculum is a major reason for the formalized tracking practices.

"... mathematics has been used as a barrier to social access, reinforcing the power structure which prevails in the societies of the Third World [and for that matter, the whole world]. No other subject in school serves so well this purpose of reinforcement of power structure as does mathematics."

–Ubiratan D'Ambrosio
 Professor Emeritus of Mathematics
 Universidad Estadual de Campinas/
 UNICAMP
 São Paulo, Brazil

• Mathematics is one of the few content areas in middle school where students are still tracked. Classroom teacher and counselor recommendations, or standardized test scores usually determine which mathematics courses a student can take. In subjects like English and history, course enrollment is not restricted; all students at each grade level take the same courses.

Isn't grouping students by ability the best way for all students to get the instruction they need?

• Course content, the type of instruction used, teacher competency, and resources vary greatly from track to track. Lower track classes tend to have content that is fragmented, often requiring students to memorize small bits of information and complete worksheets. Upper track classes, while sharing some similar characteristics, also include more opportunities for group interaction, cover more challenging material, and proceed at a faster pace with more on-task engagement.

• There is evidence that high achievers perform better in accelerated gifted and talented classes. However, many educators believe these students benefit *not* from the tracking practices but from the enriched curriculum. Enriched curriculum and instruction would also benefit students from lower track classes, if they were given the appropriate support.

• Disproportionate numbers of minority and disadvantaged students are placed in lower track classes, which often denies them equitable access to quality teachers and materials.

How can a teacher meet each student's needs if there is such a wide range of abilities in one class?

• Teachers must address a wide range of abilities in their classes whether they are tracked or not. Team teaching, cooperative learning, use of hands-on manipulatives and technology, along with appropriate assessment tools, are effective in heterogeneous mathematics classes. Curriculum that is interactive and engages students in discussions about complex high-level mathematics is also needed.

• These techniques are not enough to ensure all students have access to a rich mathematics education. The most important element in teaching a range of students is teacher and staff development. Teachers need support to examine their learned perceptions and beliefs regarding student achievement. Too often teachers and administrators believe some students lack the innate ability to achieve at the highest levels.

Is detracking the answer?

• While detracking is a beginning step towards success for all students, it is not nearly enough.

• There are several key factors necessary for successful detracking.

1) A general belief throughout the school that all students can learn.

2) The assurance to all parents that their children will receive a quality education, including encouragement to prepare for college.

3) The belief that learning improves when students listen to each other and share knowledge.

4) Continual professional development for teachers on teaching strategies for diverse groups of students, new curriculum, and communications skills.

5) If untracked courses resemble lower track ones with watered-down content, slower pace, and few resources, there will probably be no change in student achievement. Untracked mathematics should reflect high-level thinking and content.

What if I want to advance my child's mathematics track?

• Parents are an integral piece in the tracking puzzle. You must know the options available at your child's middle school, understand the future work and course implications, and assess which option is best for your child.

• Find out how to move your child from one track to another. Meet with your child's math teacher, school counselor, or principal to discuss these issues.

• Don't be intimidated by the system. Have confidence that your assessment of what your child needs is crucial.

• Hire a tutor or enroll your child in after school or summer math programs if necessary. Your local library, school, or community center should be helpful in locating assistance.

• Begin a dialogue with other middle school parents about your concerns. These communications can be both informative and supportive. Talking with other parents benefits all families.

The following potential course outlines were designed to provide middle school families with information on the high school consequences of seventh and eighth grade mathematics classes.

For your child to qualify for college, the courses taken in middle school become crucial. Now is an opportunity for you to make course adjustments to aid your child's college and career work goals. The school situation and your child's individual development will affect the exact sequence of math courses in middle and high school.

Examples of College Preparatory Sequences

Many children are ready to take algebra in the eighth grade. For these students, the following sequences provide strong mathematics preparation for college entrance.

	9th grade	10th grade	11th grade	12th grade
	Geometry	Algebra II	Pre-Calc./Trig.	Calculus[H] Calculus Calculus[AP]
8th Grade Algebra	Algebra II	Geometry	Pre-Calc./Trig	Calculus[H] Calculus Calculus[AP]
	Geometry II[H]	Algebra II	Pre-Calc./Trig	Calculus[H] Calculus Calculus[AP]
	Algebra II Geometry Algebra II Geometry[H]	Pre-Calculus	Calculus[H] Calculus Calculus[AP]	Analysis

H = Honors   **AP** = Advanced Placement

Honors **(H)** courses are high school courses where students can receive more grade points than regular classes due to advanced course content.

Advance Placement **(AP)** courses are college preparatory courses taught in high school. Students who score high enough on the **AP** exams may receive advanced placement in college or college credit.

Eighth grade algebra is not for all children. Some students will be better prepared if they begin algebra in the ninth grade. These students will begin their college preparatory sequence with eighth grade mathematics and proceed as follows.

	9th grade	10th grade	11th grade	12th grade
Algebra I	Geometry	Algebra II	Pre-Calc./Trig
Math A	Algebra	Geometry	Algebra II

8th Grade Math

It is possible for students to achieve additional grade points for college enrollment by taking Honors (H) or Advanced Placement (AP) courses. These courses can increase the traditional Grade Point Average (GPA) ceiling of 4.0 to 5.8.

Many states offer transitional mathematics courses—courses designed to provide students with skills necessary for advanced classes. However, most of these courses do not count for college entrance. Both the content and instructional strategies used in these courses should be carefully examined by parents. Many students in transitional courses receive watered-down mathematics content and find the progression to college preparatory courses difficult.

Grade Point Average (GPA) is the method high schools and colleges use to measure student achievement. To calculate Grade Point Average, each grade is given a number: A = 4 points, B = 3 points, C = 2 points, D = 1 point, F = 0 points. A student's GPA is calculated by adding the grade points for each course and dividing the total by the number of courses taken. For grades with a plus or minus, .3 is added or subtracted from the grade point. ■

Example:

Course	Grade	Grade Point
Algebra I	A–	3.7
Intro to Spanish	B	3.0
English Literature	B+	3.3
P.E.	D	1.0
History	B–	2.7
	Total	13.7
	GPA	13.7 ÷ 5 = 2.74

This student has a 2.74 Grade Point Average. He is a B– student.

Algebra

for Your Child

The questions that follow were designed to help you decide whether taking algebra in the eighth grade is appropriate for your child. If your child is in a school that requires all students to take algebra in the eighth grade, these questions will help you understand the role algebra plays in your child's mathematics education. Because each school and course are different, one answer may not be suitable for all middle school students.

As mentioned in the algebra introduction, a consensus about every student taking algebra in the eighth grade does not exist among mathematics educators. What is generally agreed is that algebraic thinking should be a strong focus at the middle school level. The bigger question is whether algebra topics appear in an integrated mathematics course or a separate algebra course. Our goal in developing the following chart is to provide questions, implications, and sources of information for your family to consider.

Finding out the answers to these questions can begin as soon as your child enters middle school. There are many factors to weigh and people to talk to before deciding. Answers to questions from the chart can be gathered during routine school interactions, back-to-school nights, and conversations with your child's teacher or school administrator.

Algebra *for Your Child*

Topic	Where to Get Information	Questions to Ask	What I Discovered	Implications
My child and mathematics	Discussions with my child, previous report cards, and teacher comments.	• Does my child like math? • What are my child's past mathematics experiences? • What kind of comments have previous teachers made regarding my child's mathematics attitude and performance? • How does he/she feel about taking algebra?		A child's mathematics confidence and attitude can impact math persistence and achievement. This is particularly true during adolescent years. Students may prefer to enroll in a less challenging course to accommodate low math confidence or the attitudes of their peers.

1

Algebra *for Your Child*

Topic	Where to Get Information	Questions to Ask	What I Discovered	Implications
Scheduling questions	Math department chair, my child's math teacher, school counselor, vice-principal, principal.	• What are the algebra course options for eighth grade? • What math course would my child take if he/she waits a year to take algebra? • What are the implications of waiting until ninth grade to take algebra? • How much experience with algebraic reasoning will my child have if we wait until the ninth grade? • How many years of college-prep mathematics courses will my child be able to take?		Math course content, instructional styles, and types of tests and evaluations vary greatly depending on a particular mathematics track. Children can think algebraically long before they manipulate algebraic symbols. If a student does not take algebra in the 8th grade, activities and curriculum which require algebraic thinking should be strongly encouraged at the middle school level. Many colleges recommend four years of high school math. Keep in mind that courses such as business math, consumer math, and math shop do not count when applying to four-year colleges or universities.

Topic	Where to Get Information	Questions to Ask	What I Discovered	Implications
Finding out about the course	Math department chair, my child's math teacher, school counselor, vice-principal, principal.	• Does the algebra program include strategies suggested by National and International Mathematics Guidelines? • Will the students need a calculator for class? • What type of activities or content does my child need to be ready for the algebra course? • What grades does my child need to get into eighth grade algebra?		The National Council of Teachers of Mathematics recommends: • activities set within a real-world context as well as those of particular interest to middle school students; • communication of math reasoning—oral or written form—with peers and others; • technology be used as a tool to allow students to concentrate on problem solving and other important mathematics concepts; • use of concrete models, group work, and on-going assessment versus one end of the year exam.

3

Topic	Where to Get Information	Questions to Ask	What I Discovered	Implications
Equity issues	Resource teacher, math department chair, my child's math teacher, school vice-principal, principal. High school math department chair and high school vice-principal are good sources of information.	• How closely does the algebra class reflect the ethnic and gender population of the school? • What type of help is available if my child needs additional support? • Does the high school advocate students taking algebra at the middle school level? • What are the high school implications if my child does not take eighth grade algebra?		Students of color, girls and second-language learners in advanced math and science courses can experience a sense of pride regarding their accomplishments, but may also feel isolated. Classroom strategies such as cooperative grouping and thematic math projects can increase student access and algebraic understanding. Extra attention and support may be necessary for students to achieve academic success. High school teachers can often provide a different perspective.

4

MATH DEPARTMENT REFERENCE SHEET

Name	Responsibilities	Contact Information	Comments
Math Teacher			
Mathematics Department Chair			
Class Advisor/Counselor			
Your Child's Teachers by Subject			

School visitation policy:

Class visitation policy:

Algebra *for Your Child*

School Staff	Responsibilities	Contact Information	Comments
Principal			
Vice Principal(s)			
Student Supervisor/Dean			
Secretary			
Resource Teachers (Bilingual Ed. Special Ed., Federal and State Special Projects)			
Community Liaison			

DISTRICT REFERENCE SHEET

Name	Responsibilities	Contact Information	Comments
School Board Members:			
Superintendent			
Associate Superintendent– Curriculum and Instruction			

Middle school builds on the experiences and skills developed in elementary school. The understanding of older concepts deepens and new concepts are taught. One way to increase student comprehension and critical thinking is by talking about mathematics. It is important for middle school children to listen to and share with parents, peers, and teachers in order to clarify their own ideas. The ability to think about mathematics in a more abstract way should particularly be encouraged at this middle school age.

As parents, you are certainly not expected to teach the content in your child's mathematics courses. However, you do play an essential instructional role by working with your child. Solving problems with your child helps solidify math concepts and skills and is invaluable in classes such as algebra, calculus, and physics.

Asking critical questions can provide a window for you to see how your child thinks mathematically. The following set of questions is designed for parents and caregivers to help their children with mathematics homework. As you work with your child, you will probably develop more questions; be sure to add them to the list. Children, as well as adults, need time to formulate their thoughts. Remember to give your child time to think about each question.

- In your own words, what is the problem about?
- Would it help to draw a diagram or make a sketch?
- What assumptions are being made?
- Is there any missing or extra information?
- Can you think of a simpler version of the problem?

- What have you tried? What steps did you take?
- Can you tell me what you know now?
- Did you check your arithmetic?
- Let's see if we can break it down. Is there a pattern?
- What are the variables or constraints in this problem?

- Did the answer make sense?
- Is there more than one answer?
- How do you know your answers are correct?
- Is there anything you overlooked?
- Did you check your arithmetic?

Note: After helping your child with the homework, share your experiences with your child's math teacher. These conversations are beneficial for your child's mathematics success and achievement.

Math Generally Covered

in Middle School

What do you remember about elementary and junior high school mathematics? Most adults think about numbers and arithmetic, usually counting, addition, subtraction, multiplication, division, fractions, percent, and word problems. Sometimes they add shapes and measuring to the list or algebra and geometry.

Is this all of mathematics? Not by any means! There are numerous other topics in mathematics. What is exciting is that many of these are appropriate for elementary and middle school.

Indeed, today's middle school students have the opportunity to learn the foundations for courses that only a few adults have been exposed to. These opportunities are reflected in the topics that are generally covered in today's middle school mathematics classes. In short, the middle school mathematics curriculum is no longer exclusively arithmetic review, as it was for many of us.

A second important circumstance that affects today's middle school mathematics curriculum is the move to teach algebra in the 8th grade. A number of school districts have been offering algebra in the 8th grade but only for advanced students. We believe that all students should experience algebraic thinking from kindergarten on. Deciding when your child is ready to take algebra is an important topic to discuss with your child's math teacher. There are many factors you will want to consider. For more information, see *Algebra for Your Child*.

The results of the *Third International Mathematics and Science Study* (TIMSS) indicate that the majority of American students start algebra a year later than students in Europe and Asia. The TIMSS report recommends that students study fewer topics each year but in more depth. If these recommendations are put in place, this would mean that middle school students would spend less time reviewing arithmetic and more time on pre-algebra and geometry concepts.

The topics mentioned below are based on the Standards prepared by the National Council of Teachers of Mathematics (NCTM). The NCTM *Standards* serve as guidelines for a strong math curriculum. They grew out of the experience and vision of the mathematics education community coupled with research on teaching and learning.

There are four general standards for all grade levels (kindergarten through grade 12) in the NCTM *Standards*. They outline the goals for the development of mathematical thinking. The middle school mathematics curriculum should include numerous and varied experiences so that students can do the following.

Overall Standards

Math as Problem Solving
- investigate mathematical ideas
- create problems from theoretical and real-world situations
- apply a variety of strategies and methods to solve problems
- confirm and interpret their results

Math as Communication
- communicate orally and in writing using diagrams and sketches to explain, interpret, and evaluate their own work

Math as Reasoning
- form and evaluate mathematical conjectures and arguments
- understand and apply reasoning processes
- validate their own thinking

Mathematical Connections
- see and apply the connections between math topics
- apply mathematical thinking to solve problems in other areas of study and everyday life, such as science and art
- value the role of mathematics in society

The following lists indicate the key topic areas and major concepts of mathematics that students should cover in grades 5 through 8. If students study algebra in the 8th grade, these topics should be covered by the end of 7th grade. Your state and local school district can provide guidelines that specify exactly when math topics will be taught in your area. The state and district lists may look somewhat different, but will probably mention most of the same topics. This information is meant to serve as a guide not an absolute timeline. Check with your child's math teacher to obtain a copy of the mathematics content for your middle school and to discuss what your child should know at each grade level.

Content Areas

Number and Arithmetic

- perform arithmetic operations and computation (addition, subtraction, multiplication, division) using whole numbers, fractions, decimals, percents, and positive and negative integers (whole numbers)

- understand and represent numbers in equivalent forms such as integers, fractions, decimals, percents, exponentials, and scientific notation

- understand and apply ratios, proportions, and percents in a wide variety of situations

- understand how to order whole numbers, fractions, decimals, and positive and negative integers

- understand how basic arithmetic operations are related to each other

- understand and apply concepts from number theory, such as prime numbers, factors, and multiples

- choose and use appropriate techniques for computation from mental arithmetic, pencil and paper, calculator, and computer

- use estimation to solve problems and determine reasonableness of results

- represent numerical relationships in one- and two-dimensional graphs

Measurement

- estimate and make measurements to describe and compare different situations

- choose appropriate units and tools to measure to the degree of accuracy required by particular situations

- understand the structure and use of different systems of measurement, such as metric and English

- understand and use the concepts of perimeter, area, volume, angle measure, capacity, weight and mass, and temperature

- develop and use formulas to solve measurement problems including those requiring knowledge of perimeter, area, and volume

Geometry

- identify, describe, compare, and classify geometric figures including triangles, quadrilaterals, polygons, circles, and three-dimensional figures

- represent and solve problems using geometric models

- understand and apply geometric properties and relationships including properties of triangles, quadrilaterals, circles (Pythagorean Theorem)

- develop an appreciation of geometry as a means of describing the physical world

Patterns and Functions

- create, describe, extend, and analyze a wide variety of both numerical and geometric patterns

- describe and represent relationships with tables, graphs, and rules or functions (a function is a rule that has only one output for each input)

- analyze functional relationships to explain how a change in one quantity affects the other

- use patterns, tables, and functions to represent and solve problems

Statistics

- systematically collect, organize, and describe data (information)

- construct, read, and interpret tables, charts, and graphs

- make inferences and convincing arguments that are based on data analysis

- evaluate arguments that are based on data analysis

- develop an appreciation for statistical methods as powerful tools for decision making

Probability

- devise and carry out experiments that simulate real-world situations to determine probabilities

- appreciate and understand the power of comparing a theoretical probability model with experimental results using mathematical expectation

- list all possibilities for a particular situation in order to determine probabilities

- make predictions based on experimental and theoretical probabilities

- develop an appreciation for the use of probability in the real world

Algebra

- understand and apply the concepts of variable, expression, and equations

- translate or represent situations, number patterns, tables, graphs, and verbal rules into algebraic equations and explore the interrelationships of these representations

- analyze tables, graphs, and equations to identify properties and relationships, such as: when x increases, y decreases

- understand and use algebraic methods to solve and apply linear equations

- be familiar with the concept of inequalities and the idea of nonlinear equations

- apply algebraic methods to solve real-world problems

In addition, to the content list for the middle school grades, most teachers emphasize three concepts that reoccur in grades 5 to 8. They are the following.

Proportional Reasoning

Proportional relationships represent the connection between two quantities or the representation of one quantity as a certain portion of another.

Example: at a sale with a discount of 25%, the discount is ¼ or 25% of the original price.

Example: we say the ratio of the length of a meter to a centimeter is 100: 1; that is, a meter is 100 times as long as a centimeter.

Example: scale drawings represent proportional relationships between the drawing and the real objects.

Multiple Representations

There are often a variety of ways to present mathematical information.

Example: when we say we have half of something, we can also say that we have ²⁄₄, ³⁄₆, 0.5, or 50% of that item.

Example: an algebraic equation such as $y = x + 1$ can be also represented in a function table or as a line on a graph as illustrated.

Patterns and Generalization

People often call mathematics the science of patterns. Observing patterns helps to generalize information so that it is easier to use or can help interpret what is happening.

Example: in the table above the graph, you can discover the pattern that each y is one more than each x. The equation $y = x + 1$ is a way to determine what will occur for any number (x) that is used in the pattern and record it mathematically. ■

x	y
1	2
2	3
5	6
8	9

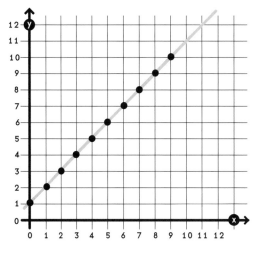

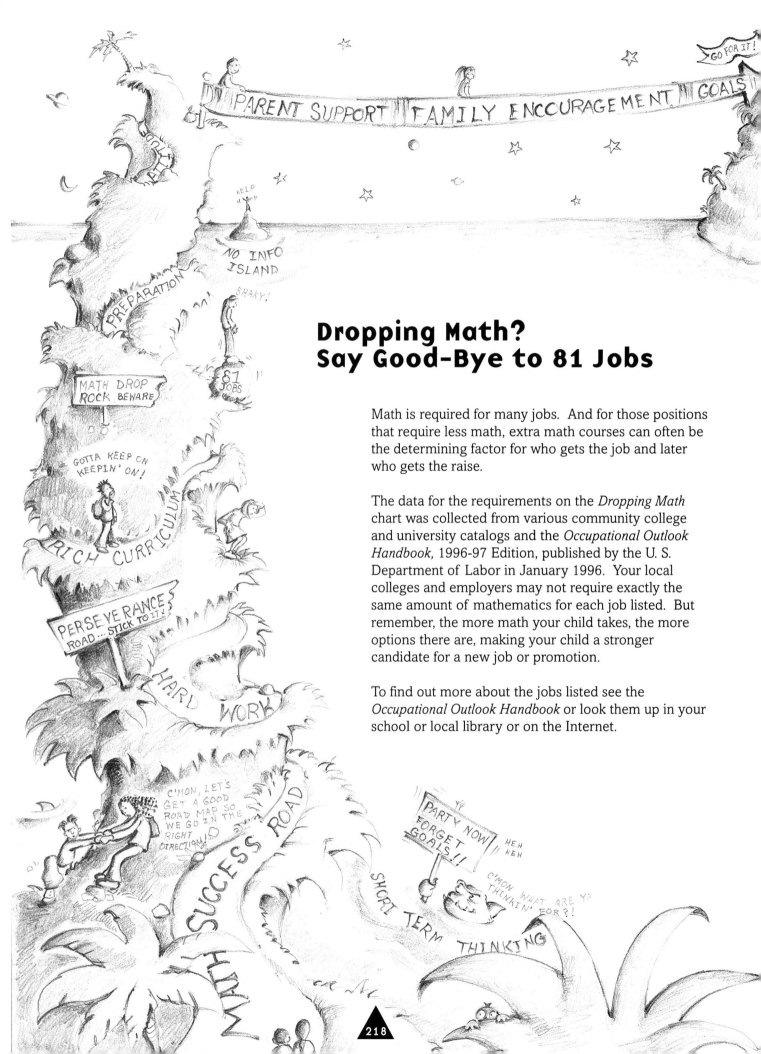

Dropping Math?
Say Good-Bye to 81 Jobs

Math is required for many jobs. And for those positions that require less math, extra math courses can often be the determining factor for who gets the job and later who gets the raise.

The data for the requirements on the *Dropping Math* chart was collected from various community college and university catalogs and the *Occupational Outlook Handbook,* 1996-97 Edition, published by the U. S. Department of Labor in January 1996. Your local colleges and employers may not require exactly the same amount of mathematics for each job listed. But remember, the more math your child takes, the more options there are, making your child a stronger candidate for a new job or promotion.

To find out more about the jobs listed see the *Occupational Outlook Handbook* or look them up in your school or local library or on the Internet.

Dropping Math Alphabetical Occupations List

a. Four years of high school math required + college calculus and more

Actuary
Applied and Pure Mathematician
Astronomer
Biochemist
Chemist
College Math Professor
Computer Systems Analyst
Engineer
Geologist
Math Teacher
Meteorologist
Operations Research Analyst
Physicist
Statistician

b. Four years high school math required + college calculus and/or statistics

Architect
Biologist
Dentist
Economist
Forester/Conservation Scientist
Optometrist
Pharmacist
Physician
Electronic Technician
Geographer
Veterinarian

c. Three to four years of high school math recommended, applied math and statistics are important

Accountant, Certified Public
Audiologist
Cartographer/Map Maker
Computer Programmer
Cost Estimator
Dental Hygienist
Drafter
Electronic Technician
Elementary Teacher
Landscape Architect
Lawyer

Loan and Insurance Underwriters
Occupational and Physical Therapist
Pilots and Flight Engineers
Property Appraiser
Psychologist
Public Health Nurse
Registered Nurse
Sociologist
Speech Therapist
Stock Broker
Surveyor
Urban Planner

d. Two years of high school math required, more is better

Agricultural Technician
Building and Construction
  Inspectors
Data Processor
Electrician
Graphic Artist
Health Record Administrator
Insurance Claims and Policy
  Processing Clerks

Interior Designer
Loan and Credit
  Checkers
Machinist
Pharmacy Assistant
Statistical Clerk
Tool and Die Maker

e. Two years of high school math recommended, practical math is important

Animal Care Technician
Bank Teller
Bookkeeper
Bricklayer/Stonemason
Carpenter
Cashier
Commercial Driver
Computer Technologist
Jeweler
Mail Carrier

Mechanic
Medical Equipment
  Maintenance Technician
Order Clerk
Plumber
Respiratory Technologist
Stock and Inventory Clerks
Travel Agents
Weigher, Measurer, Checker
Welder
X-ray Technician

Dropping Math? *Say Good-Bye to 81 Jobs*

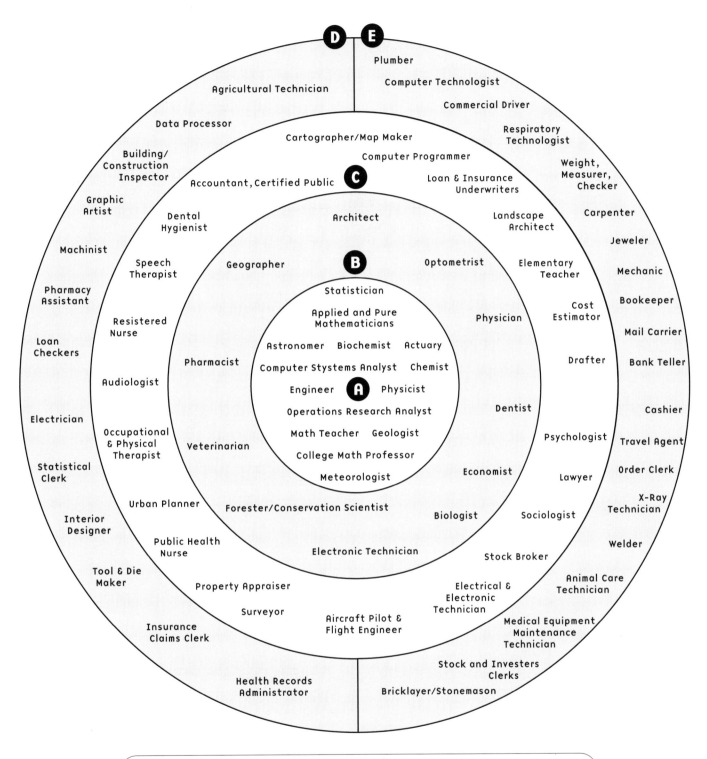

D **E**

Plumber

Agricultural Technician

Computer Technologist

Commercial Driver

Data Processor

Respiratory Technologist

Cartographer/Map Maker

Building/ Construction Inspector

Computer Programmer

C

Weight, Measurer, Checker

Accountant, Certified Public

Loan & Insurance Underwriters

Graphic Artist

Dental Hygienist

Architect

Landscape Architect

Carpenter

Machinist

B

Jeweler

Speech Therapist

Geographer

Optometrist

Elementary Teacher

Mechanic

Pharmacy Assistant

Statistician

Physician

Cost Estimator

Bookeeper

Resistered Nurse

Applied and Pure Mathematicians

Mail Carrier

Loan Checkers

Pharmacist

Astronomer Biochemist Actuary

Drafter

Bank Teller

Computer Stystems Analyst Chemist

Audiologist

Engineer **A** Physicist

Cashier

Electrician

Operations Research Analyst

Dentist

Travel Agent

Occupational & Physical Therapist

Math Teacher Geologist

Veterinarian

College Math Professor

Psychologist

Order Clerk

Statistical Clerk

Meteorologist

Economist

Lawyer

X-Ray Technician

Urban Planner

Forester/Conservation Scientist

Interior Designer

Biologist

Sociologist

Welder

Public Health Nurse

Electronic Technician

Stock Broker

Tool & Die Maker

Property Appraiser

Animal Care Technician

Surveyor

Electrical & Electronic Technician

Insurance Claims Clerk

Aircraft Pilot & Flight Engineer

Medical Equipment Maintenance Technician

Stock and Investers Clerks

Health Records Administrator

Bricklayer/Stonemason

Legend
A - 4 years of high school math required + college calculus and more
B - 4 years of high school math required + college calculus and/or statistics
C - 3 to 4 years of high school math recommended, applied math and statistics are important
D - 2 years high school math required, more is better
E - 2 years high school math recommended, practical math is important

Keep in mind that courses such as business math, consumer math, and math shop do not count when applying to four-year colleges or universities.

Uninformed Decisions

Taking the appropriate courses in high school, especially in mathematics and science, opens the door to numerous options for future work and study. On the other hand, dropping math and science as soon as possible closes the doors to these opportunities. (See *Dropping Math?* on page 218.)

Data from a 1995 survey conducted for the National Action Council for Minorities in Engineering (NACME) indicate that few families realize the importance of high school course choices and their impact on future schooling. This activity demonstrates the need for more communication about these topics. See if it helps you think of more things to find out about and share with other families.

WHAT'S THE MATH CONNECTION?

Importance of middle and high school math courses for college study and work; importance of parent and teacher support of mathematics for students grades 5 to 12.

How

If You Are Working at Home

• Look over the questions on the next page. Choose two or three and make a guess about their answers.

• Discuss why the questions are important.

• Look up the answers. Do they surprise you? Why? Why not?

• Discuss what happens at your school about these issues. What can you do as a family to get more information about math and science requirements in high school and college. Whom could you ask at school? Could you get information at the local library or on the Internet? How?

• Try *College Catalog Information* on p. 226.

In a FAMILY MATH Class Session

• To prepare for using this activity in your class, make a set of the questions. Write each question on a separate card (or paper). Make duplicates as necessary, so that there is one card for each person. Laminate the cards if you plan to use them again.

• Make one answer sheet for each person. Or have them make their own on scratch paper.

• Give each person an answer sheet.

• Tape a question on each person's back, without letting them see the question.

• People will estimate the answers to the questions on each other's backs, without letting the other person know what the question is. Each person will collect estimates from five different people, recording them on his or her answer sheet.

• After getting five answers, each participant finds the average or mean of the five estimates (add the five estimates and divide by five). Then, they can read their questions.

• When everyone is done, you are ready to collect the averages for each question. Ask one of the people who has Question 1 to read it and give the average of their answers. Collect that information from everyone else who has Question 1.

• Estimate the average of averages and discuss if that average seems reasonable. Then give the actual answer from the survey and discuss the importance of the question.

• Continue with the other questions.

• Finish with a more general discussion about the issues that the questions raise and how the school, parents, and other significant adults can work together to provide better communication about these matters.

• Give out copies of the questions for participants to share with other families.

• Do the *College Catalog Information* activity as a follow up.

Uninformed Decisons Questions

NACME includes African American, Latino, and American Indian students when they refer to "minority" students. Wording in the questions and answers reflects that of the report.

1. What percent of parents have never been informed about the decisions their children must make about future math courses and the implications?

2. What percent of students who have options regarding math say they make the decisions by themselves about the courses they will pursue?

3. What percent of minority 9th to 11th graders think that being a scientist would be interesting?

4. Over half of all students grades 5 to 11 plan to drop math as soon as it is not required. What percent of African American students plan to drop math and science at the first opportunity?

5. What percent of minority students nationwide graduate from high school with the prerequisite mathematics and science courses necessary to begin an engineering or other science-based college major?

6. What percent of minority 9th to 11th graders think they can take any class at any time without completing prerequisite courses?

7. Two-thirds of non-minority 9th to 11th graders have been encouraged by their teachers to take advanced classes. What percent of minority students have had this encouragement?

8. What percent of students grades 5–8 say their friends or one or more significant adults in their lives (parents or guardians, teachers, family members, counselors, school principals) have discouraged them from succeeding in math and science courses?

9. Seventeen percent of 5-8th graders say they have been discouraged from succeeding in math by their parents. What percent of parents say that they have discouraged their children in this age group?

10. What percent of students believe that having a special talent for math is **not** important for success in math and science?

11. What percent of students say their peers stop taking math and science classes because schools do not offer enough of these courses?

12. Forty-eight percent of Asian and white students understand that not taking advanced math courses will limit their future academic options. What is the percentage for African American students?

13. Less than half of all 9th to 11th graders plan to take advanced math classes such as Algebra II or Trig. What percent of African American students this age say they are interested in college level math?

14. What percent of students who plan to stop taking math as soon as possible want to study science subjects in college?

Answers

The questions and answers in this activity are based on a summary of "Uninformed Decisions: A Survey of Children and Parents about Math and Science," by Robert Leitman, Katherine Binns and Akhil Unni that appeared in the *NACME Research Letter*, Vol. 5, Number 1, June 1995.

1. 93%

2. 79%
Sixty-six percent of the parents surveyed said their children made these decisions by themselves.

3. 77%
The figure is 65% for non-minorities. Seventy percent of minority students this age think being an engineer would be interesting, while 59% percent of non-minority students feel the same.

4. 63%
Sixty percent Latino and 58 percent American Indians plan to drop these courses as soon as possible.

5. 6%
The percent for non-minority students is 12.

6. 20%
Sixteen percent of non-minority 9th to 11th graders believe this.

7. 50%

8. 50%
Nineteen percent of these students have been discouraged by friends; 17% by parents or guardians; 15% by teachers; 13% by family members; 11% by counselors; and 10% by principals.

9. 1%

10. 16%
Eighty-one percent of students say having a special talent is at least somewhat important in succeeding at math. Older students are more likely to believe this (86% vs 77%). Eighty-seven percent of students who have discussed math options with an adult feel a special talent is important, compared with 80% of those who have not discussed math options with an adult.

11. 39%
Forty percent of minority students in grades 9 –11 say this compared with 32% non-minority students.

12. 27%
The percent for Latino students is 35%, and 29% for American Indian students.

13. 78%
Forty-six percent of African American students this age say they are very interested in taking college level math.

14. 35%
One-fourth of those who are not interested in or have not chosen advanced math and science courses in high school want to study science subjects in college. ■

College Catalog Information

MATERIALS

pencil and paper

college catalogs

WHAT'S THE MATH CONNECTION?

Course requirements and prerequisites for community college and college majors.

College catalogs provide information about the requirements for majors, degrees, and certificates. Reading these catalogs and obtaining all of the information needed for enrollment and subsequent course requirements can be challenging. Unfortunately, this information is not always presented in a clear manner.

A good strategy is to begin the process at the middle school level. It is helpful to explore options at this time while there are no deadlines to meet. It is also important to get familiar with college catalog information while mathematics and science courses are still open to your child. Many course opportunities will be closed if your family waits until your child's sophomore or junior year in high school.

The following investigation provides a format for your family to research college catalogs and the pertinent mathematics information contained in them.

How

• Work with a partner or family member.

Colleges and Universities
• Get a college or university catalog. Find the section that lists the majors.

• Choose two majors to look up, one that you think will require math and one that might not.

• Study the requirements for the math-based major to find out what courses are required and their *prerequisites*. (A *prerequisite* is a course that must be completed before you can enter another course. Sometimes, you are allowed to take the two courses at the same time, concurrently; however, you almost always need to get special permission to do this.)

• How many math courses are required? What are they?

• Look up each math and science class in the alphabetical course listing to see if they require a math prerequisite that does not appear on the requirement list.

College Catalog Information

Community colleges are often referred to as two-year institutions. They usually offer two types of programs. One type leads to an Associates of Arts (A.A.) degree, technical diploma, or certificate in fields such as electronics, word processing, welding, accounting, and carpentry. The other program prepares students to transfer to four-year colleges. Most community colleges require that you are a resident of the state and have received a high school diploma, GED (General Education Diploma), or similar state diploma or proficiency certificate. Special circumstances for admission are usually listed in the front of their catalogs.

Colleges and universities are called four-year institutions. This means that a full-time student could graduate in four years. They offer Bachelors of Arts (B.A.) and Bachelors of Science (B.S.) degrees in a range of undergraduate majors such as anthropology, sociology, chemistry, and engineering.

• Check to see if there are any general math requirements for graduation, no matter your major.

• Look up the entrance requirements for the school. What are the math and science requirements. What does this mean for your child's high school schedule?

• Check out the requirements for the non-math-based major.

• Find another college or university catalog and look up the same information for the two majors you chose.

• Are the requirements the same?

• Which catalog was easier to read?

• Share your results with the whole group.

Community Colleges
• Go through the same procedure for two community college catalogs.

• Do both catalogs have information about majors that can transfer to four-year colleges and universities?

Note: We use the word *college* to refer to many different kinds of schools that you can attend after high school. They can have different entrance requirements and give different kinds of degrees, diplomas, and certificates. The explanations given here are meant to serve only as a general description of these institutions. ■

> **Extension**
>
> • Check to see if the college and university catalogs give information about the requirements to enter programs for graduate degrees or professional programs, such as architecture, business, medicine, or law. If not, find out how to obtain that information.

83 percent of students who take algebra and geometry enroll in college—more than double the percentage (36%) of students who do not take these courses.

Community Update, No. 53, January 1998, U.S. Department of Education, P. 1.

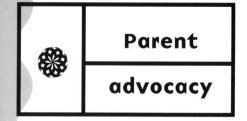
Useful Math Survey

How

The Survey

• Read over the list of math skills on the Survey Sheet with your family.

• Discuss examples that illustrate the use of each skill. Prepare to explain what is meant by the different skills when you are collecting data. Add any skills that you think are important to include. Check out your ideas with another group or the whole class.

• During the week, interview at least five people for the survey. Get different family members to help. Use the Survey Sheet if you think it will be helpful.

• Before you begin, make a prediction with your family about which skills will be mentioned most frequently and which will be mentioned least often. Bring your data to share and discuss at the next class.

Useful Math Survey Follow-Up
• Discuss the information you collected with your family and the others in your group. Were you surprised by the results? Were they similar to your predictions?

• Which math skills were most frequently mentioned?
Was there any topic that was mentioned by everyone or almost everyone?

• What other skills did people say were important at work?

• What were some of the most interesting comments they made?

• Pick out three or four of the most interesting points from your group and be ready to share with the whole class.

Sample Interview
Hi, I'm researching mathematics used on the job for our FAMILY MATH class.

We want to find out what mathematics is most important in the workplace as well as the variety of math used at work. Would you spend about five minutes answering our survey questions?

Please indicate which of the following math skills you use at work. Let me know if you would like me to explain or clarify what we mean by any of the skills on the list. Are there any other skills that you have found particularly important in your job? Are there any general comments you would like to make?

Would you like a copy of our class report when all of the data is collected? ■

> **Extension**
>
> • Organize and make a class record or graph of all of the data collected.

Useful Math Survey

Job Title	Math Taken in School	Mathematics used on the Job	Other Useful Skills	Comments

Math Topics
algebra
averaging
calculators (use of)
computer (use of for spreadsheets or calculations)
computer programming
coordinate graphing
decimals
estimation
formulas
fractions
geometry
measurement
percent
probability
ratio and proportion
statistical graphs (creating and interpreting)
trigonometry

There is no one way to organize a FAMILY MATH Middle School class series. The class can be taught by parents, teachers, administrators, and community members. The belief in the importance of family involvement in education and the desire to share mathematics in a nonthreatening and enthusiastic way are the only requirements. The suggestions below are meant to serve as guidelines. But remember, you are the expert on what will work best in your community.

WORKING WITH A PARTNER

Many teachers, parents, and community members have led FAMILY MATH class series on their own. However, everyone who has worked with a partner says they would never do it alone. Partners share the responsibilities. They help make decisions about what to do and how to do it. Partners can work behind the scenes to arrange the next activity while you are "on." Most importantly, partners can share the excitement with you. If you have the opportunity to team-lead your FAMILY MATH classes, we encourage you to do so. If there is no one available, start small and see if you can recruit a partner from the first class.

WHO SHOULD COME?

Grade Level

All of the activities in this book are appropriate for families whose children are in grades 5 through 8. You may want to focus on your own grade level or offer a series for all of the middle grades in your school or community. Some leaders will want to include the whole family and invite younger and older siblings as well. These leaders adjust by selecting activities that work for a larger age range or spending part of the time in grade level groupings.

WHEN IS THE BEST TIME?

Scheduling

There is more interest in FAMILY MATH during the fall and winter months than in spring. Avoid holidays, school vacations, and other unusually busy times. We recommend having two-hour sessions once a week for six successive weeks. Try to pick a block of time when you can set the classes at the same time each week for the whole series. Early evening classes are very successful. Some series are offered on Saturday mornings. School afternoons rarely work well for parents. Before you set a time for your class, you may want to send home a recruitment flyer including a return portion for parents and caregivers to indicate their preferred time. See the sample form on page 243.

I learned different ways of getting math ideas across.
You can use props or tools to visually make your point.

FAMILY MATH Participant

Location

WHERE IS THE BEST PLACE?

School classrooms, libraries, community centers, churches, and science centers are all good locations for a FAMILY MATH class series. You will want to consider the following:

- Is there a charge for the facility?
- Are there enough tables and chairs for everyone and for extra activities?
- Is there a separate room for baby-sitting?
- Is there ample parking?
- Is the location safe at night?

Recruitment

HOW DO I GET FAMILIES TO COME?

Recruitment can be the easiest or the hardest part of a class series. If your community has high parent involvement, you may have more people interested than you can handle. If the parents in your community do not attend school functions regularly, you may want to recruit through community centers or churches. You can also invite families from other schools. In either case, you will want to work with parent and community leaders to help expand the program.

It is easy to be satisfied with reaching the families that respond to notices sent home announcing your class series. However, FAMILY MATH was developed by the EQUALS program that works to increase access and success in mathematics for every student. We particularly encourage you to take extra efforts to reach families who have not been involved with school activities in the past.

Reaching Out to All Families

Many families do not feel welcome in the schools. Alienation can be caused by a variety of barriers such as unfriendly attitudes of the school staff, unpleasant personal school experiences, and language differences. Added to these difficulties is the fact that middle school age students might not want their parents involved. However, parents want to help their children succeed. The secret of recruiting less involved families often lies in personal contact by you, the school staff, and involved community members.

Voices of Experience

Some successful strategies have been to offer:

- homework credit or extra credit;
- door prizes and raffles;
- baby-sitting or activities for younger siblings;
- student involvement in explaining some of the activities;
- refreshments, such as pizza, donated by local businesses.

Demonstrating activities in the classroom, making announcements in community and church bulletins, and having students present part of the class are great ideas. In some areas radio spots, newspaper announcements, and notices in local stores also work. Personal and phone invitations are most effective. You will develop a set of recruitment strategies that work best for your situation.

Adults and Children

It is particularly important that you make clear that NO CHILD MAY ATTEND WITHOUT AN ADULT. Adults may attend with or without a child. If you do not maintain this rule, you will find yourself with a tutorial session for a lot of students who want extra help. This is not the purpose of FAMILY MATH.

FINANCIAL SUPPORT

Finances

Make a list of projected expenses to be sure you can cover the costs. Although you can charge a "per family" fee, such fees should be kept as small as possible. Don't be afraid to ask for donations of all kinds—from principals, businesses, philanthropic organizations, parent groups, or the local grocery store. Most people find the idea of FAMILY MATH very exciting and will be willing to contribute materials or money.

Expenses

Here are some expenses to think about:
- handouts and materials for families—about $1 per family per week;
- rent—try to get space free in a school, community center, or church;
- refreshments—look for donations from the community or families;
- your own time—much of your time will be donated, but you may be able to arrange a small honorarium through a local adult school, your district, or a special grant.

SETTING UP FOR THE CLASSES

Preparation

See the *Planning Check Sheet* on page 245. Double check that you have all of the materials and enough handouts prepared. Be sure that you have a comfortable room arrangement that allows participants to hear you and each other.

Set-up

Give yourself plenty of time to set up. Be ready for the early birds. You may need to arrive an hour or more beforehand for the first session. Provide name tags to help everyone get to know each other. Have juice and coffee and tea available.

You will need to maintain a formal attendance list with addresses and phone numbers, so you can keep in contact with the families. You can still use informal ways to keep attendance, such as having people sign in on a Venn diagram or graph and transferring that information to your list. Some classes set up buddy families to provide a way for families to work together.

THEY'RE ALL HERE—NOW WHAT?

Welcoming

The atmosphere you establish is the most important part of the classes. Your actions as well as your words can convey a message of welcome. A nonthreatening, comfortable environment is key to the success of the program. It gives adults and children the confidence to take risks, try something new and make mistakes, and learn from them. The activities will generate discussion. Encourage participants to ask questions.

They say that mathematics has great beauty, that it can be learned and enjoyed by everyone. When people begin to concentrate on the excitement and fun of doing mathematics rather than getting the one right answer, your classes will be a success.

Class Openers

FAMILY MATH classes should begin with one or more opener activities that require little or no explanation. Start the class at the designated time with families or table groups working on the openers as they arrive. Then, any families who are late can come in and get involved without feeling uncomfortable.

Some of the activities that work particularly well as openers have the **icon**. You can also use the first steps of a longer activity as openers. Then begin a class with a discussion of what people observed and learned as a lead into the activity.

While families are working at the openers, provide encouragement and suggestions where needed. Make observations of points to be discussed later. When you close this part of the class, discuss the mathematics in the openers, why they were chosen, and how they fit into the curriculum.

Program Description

At the first meeting, you will want to explain the FAMILY MATH program.

FAMILY MATH is the "daughter" of EQUALS, a program that has looked at access and equity issues in mathematics education since 1977. FAMILY MATH and its leaders address mathematics equity issues in the following ways:
- reaching out to families and educators in the community;
- welcoming families from all backgrounds to their classes;
- believing in all students and expecting each student to do well in math;
- providing materials that are designed for math success;
- providing translators and materials in languages other than English;
- supporting parents and caregivers in helping their children with math;
- helping parents, caregivers, and students think about and plan for future learning and work.

Make introductions and give an overview of the series of classes. Explain there will be some times when the students and adults work separately. You may also want to announce which night will have the role model session, so that families can invite friends and siblings to attend.

Activities

For the first activity on the first night, pick something that is based on number skills or an activity with an obvious connection to learning algebra. You want something that addresses mathematics that the adults remember as important. With less familiar math topics, talk about the opportunities students have to learn more mathematics than we (parents) did. These "new" topics lay the foundations for algebra, geometry, and other more advanced mathematics courses—as well as for more career options. Each activity has information about the mathematics involved and many include career connections.

Plan for Success

Save the most challenging activities for later classes. You want everyone to be successful, especially in the beginning. Many adults are intimidated by math. Just coming to the class can be a big step for them. You want to be sure that they come back next week!

Activity Directions	Introduce each new activity with clear directions. Model procedures and game rules with the whole group or a subgroup that others can easily observe. Give oral and written directions. Use illustrations as often as possible. But don't worry if a family doesn't "follow the rules;" they might have found an interesting variation.
Discussion	After each activity take time for discussion and questions. Ask participants how they approached the activity, what strategies they tried, and which ones seemed to work best. Ask several families to explain how they reached their results. Be sure to ask what mathematics is involved in the activity, but be ready to contribute ideas to get started. Include information about connections to future math courses and jobs.
Lesson Plans	See the generic lesson plan on page 244.
Parent Talk	It is useful to have some segments of the classes devoted to meeting separately with the adults. The students can work with your partner or continue an activity during this time. These sessions can run from 15 to 30 minutes. You probably won't schedule them for each class, but try to fit them in for at least half of the classes.
	Parent Talk is particularly important at the middle school level, because there are so many crucial issues for children at this age. With the onset of adolescence, middle school students often wonder (and worry) about "The Future." The students are also going through many changes including a new school structure and having several teachers.
	Parents may have specific questions about what courses their children should take, and about college and the job market. You don't have to be an expert to address the issues. The group can generate a list of resources or invite a guest to provide more information. Whatever the topic, be sure that everyone has a chance to be heard. Adults will appreciate this time to ask questions and share information and strategies with each other.

CLOSING

Handouts	At the end of class, review the activities and give out instructions for all the activities done in that class. Be sure to give the families copies of all of the activities they have done. The copyright for all materials in this book is held by the Regents of the University of California. You are granted permission to reproduce activities for the families in your classes. You may also want to supply materials such as dice, beans, squares, spinners, and playing boards for the families to take home.

Homework

Give any special reminders about trying things at home during the week. Encourage families to keep journals of their experiences as they explore mathematical ideas at home and in class. Let them know that you look forward to seeing them at the next session.

MORE ON ACTIVITIES AND TIMING

Topics

The activities in this book emphasize number, number sense, algebraic thinking, and logical thinking. The activities have been chosen because they promote problem solving and mathematical reasoning. They involve the use of concrete materials and foster discussion. You will find many that overlap with spatial reasoning. When you plan your classes you may want one topic as a theme or activities from a variety of topics.

Guided Activities

Check to see that the adults and children have enough prior knowledge to understand the basis of the activity. Some new ideas might need to be introduced before beginning these activities. They are indicated with the **icon.** Longer activities will need more input or guidance on your part. In some cases, you may want to start an activity one week and finish it the next with a related homework assignment in between.

Games

Activities that are games are marked with the **icon.** A second icon indicates whether they work better as Openers or Guided Activities.

MAKING CAREER CONNECTIONS

Having a role model panel can demystify some of the questions about future choices. We recommend a panel of from one to four role models working in a range of math-related fields from the skilled trades to business to research scientists. College students majoring in math- or science-based fields are also excellent role models, particularly if they attended schools in the community.

Role Models

Start the role model session with an opener such as reports from the *Useful Math Survey.* When the panel begins, ask each role model to talk for five minutes about the work they do, the field they study, and how they decided on that field. Suggest that they discuss how parents, teachers, and other significant adults influenced their choices. Almost all role models who speak to us wish they had taken more mathematics courses. Hold questions until all of the panelists have spoken.

To find role models, ask members of the class and friends for suggestions. Contact organizations such as the Society of Women Engineers and the career center at local colleges.

OTHER HOME LANGUAGES

Non-English-speaking Families

FAMILY MATH has served as an excellent vehicle to reach families who do not speak English at home. It provides a comfortable way for them to become involved with school and to learn the importance of mathematics in this culture. If the class leader does not speak the families' languages, a translator (or translators) will be needed. Some leaders ask the translator to sit with the families, do the activities with them, and answer questions as they come up. Check with the translator frequently. There may be many questions since our approach may differ dramatically from math instruction in other countries. Be sure to allow time for these conversational translations to be completed before moving on too quickly. It is important to provide translations of the handouts if at all possible.

EVALUATION

Evaluations

It may seem strange to evaluate your informal FAMILY MATH classes, but is useful to know how your activities are going, which ones the adults like best, which ones the children like best, what they are learning, and how you might improve the class.

Why should I evaluate?
- For my own information, to help me to improve the class
- For administrators, school board, community interest
- For potential supporters, who like to know what they're supporting

What could I evaluate?
- Who came? Why did they come? What do they hope to accomplish? Who does or doesn't come back? Why do or don't they return?
- How is the class going? Are people enjoying it? Are my presentations and explanations clear? Am I making the connections that people need?
- What are people taking home from the class? Are they more positive about math and about their children's math education?
- What are people doing between classes? Do they use any of the activities? Do they find more math activities in their family lives? Are they getting more involved with their children's math education?
- What are some long-term outcomes of the class? Are parents more involved with the school? Are parents learning more math themselves? Are children more interested in math?

How can I evaluate?

- Informal comments—begin the class with introductions and a question, like: "How did you hear about the class?" "Why did you come?" "Did you try any activities from last week?"

- Journals—ask parents to keep notes of the classes in journals where they also record math activities and reflections they have between classes. Borrow these journals to read at the end of the sessions.

- Checklists—list the activities you've presented by name and ask parents to rate them (didn't attend or don't remember, liked it, didn't like it, tried it at home, plan to try it sometime, don't plan to try it).

- Follow-up strategies—talk to children's teachers, talk to children, have a follow-up meeting with parents.

Any other advice?

- Respect parents' and children's privacy; don't let others see their comments; gather only data that you plan to use; ask questions for a reason; and try to act on people's recommendations if you agree that they're sound.

- Listening carefully is one of the best evaluation techniques available!

BEST OF LUCK!

We hope this section on how to set up a Middle School FAMILY MATH series has been helpful to you. We have tried to give you enough information to proceed without overwhelming you with ideas. We'd love to hear how your class went.

If you have questions or comments, please contact us at:

FAMILY MATH Network
(510) 642-1823 or (510) 784-0941
FAX: (510) 643-5757
Email: equals@uclink4.berkeley.edu

FAMILY MATH

Learn
- How to help your child with math
- What your child will learn in math this year
- What math courses lead to more career options
- How to make math more fun

Take Home
- Materials; activities and games; career information

Meet
- Women and men who use math in their jobs

For more information call:

_____   _____
(NAME)   (PHONE)

Please return the bottom of this sheet to:

_____
(ADDRESS)

_____

_____

Yes, I'm interested in FAMILY MATH.

NAME

ADDRESS

PHONE

BEST TIME TO CALL

CHILD'S NAME

CHILD'S GRADE

CHILD'S MATH TEACHER

BEST TIME FOR ME TO ATTEND A FAMILY MATH CLASS:

	WEEKDAYS	❑ 3:00–5:00
		❑ 6:00–8:00
	SATURDAYS	❑ 10:00–12:00

FIRST CHOICE: _____   SECOND CHOICE: _____

❑ I cannot attend a FAMILY MATH class series now, but keep me on your mailing list.

Generic Middle School FAMILY MATH Lesson Plan

Time	Activities	Materials and Handouts
10–15 min.	Openers	Opener Materials Opener Handouts
5–20 min.	Introduction/ Overview of Evening Go over Openers Discuss last weeks "homework"	
20–30 min.	Activity	Activity Materials Activity Handouts
5 min.	Discussion	
20–30 min.	Activity	Activity Materials Activity Handouts
5 min.	Discussion	
20–30 min.	Activity	Activity Materials Activity Handouts
5 min.	Discussion	
5–10 min.	Review Activities Questions Specify things to try at home Comment Cards for Evaluation	Blank Cards for Comments

Notes
- You may want to discuss the "homework" later in the class.
- You may want to give all of the handouts and take-home materials out at the end of the class.
- You may want to let some activities run as long as 45 minutes.
- Discussion times will vary.
- Your schedule will change when you include Parent Talk and Role Model sessions.

FAMILY MATH Planning Check Sheet

Things to do before class:

When	What
1 or 2 months before class	❏ Decide on time and place. ❏ Decide on grade levels. ❏ Make arrangements with principal, district office, custodian and the like.
About 6 weeks before class	❏ Begin recruiting. (Much earlier than eight weeks and people may forget, and less than three weeks doesn't leave enough time for parents to plan.)
1 or 2 weeks before each class	❏ Finalize class curriculum. ❏ Begin to gather needed materials. ❏ Prepare masters for handouts. ❏ Line up child care if appropriate.
About 2 weeks before the role panel	❏ Select date and line up role models for model career panel.
1 week before class	❏ Run off handouts for first week (guess on enrollment). ❏ Double-check room availability. ❏ Send home reminder notices.
1 day to 2 hours before class	❏ Triple-check room arrangements. ❏ Arrange furniture the way you like it. ❏ Make coffee, tea, etc., arrangements ❏ Set up openers, sign in sheet, and other materials.
When class begins	❏ Relax, it's going to be wonderful!

Some Good Middle School Activities from the Original FAMILY MATH Book

Activity	Topics	Page
A Working Day	Careers	261
Aunt Bebe's Costly Calculations	Calculators/Number Sense	240
Pico, Fermi, Bagels	Number Sense	64
Calculator Paths (x and -)	Calculators/Number Sense	235
Coordinate Tic-Tac-Toe	Coordinate Graphing	196
Coordinates I and II	Coordinate Graphing	192/194
Cut-A-Card*	Spatial Reasoning	190
Double Digit*	Number Sense	111
Gorp	Ratios and Proportions	136
Graphing Information*	Statistics	145
How Long Is a Name?	Statistics	148
Hurkle	Coordinate Graphing/Logic	198
Judy's Fractions	Number Sense	125
Lid Ratios*	Measurement	97
Lost Number	Calculators/Number Sense	249
Lost Rules	Calculators/Algebra	247
Magnified Inch	Measurement	86
Means Justify the End	Statistics	147
Nimble Calculator*	Calculators/Logical Thinking	47
Number Line Rectangles	Number Sense/Measurement	115
Palindromes	Number Sense	214
Pentasquare Activities	Spatial Reasoning	188
Pseudo-Monopoly	Percents/Logical Thinking	251
Rainbow Logic	Spatial Reasoning/Logical Thinking	62
Random Walk II	Probability	164
Reverse Double Digit*	Number Sense	113
Rolling Records* – Steps I* & II	Probability	156/158
Save Twenty*	Number Sense/Probabilty	70
Shopping Spree	Calculators/Estimation	49
Tangram Shape Sheet*	Spatial Reasoning	42
Target Addition*	Number Sense/Logical Thinking	32
Tax Collector	Number Sense/Logical Thinking	67
Ten Card Arrangement*	Logical Thinking	66
Three Bean Salads*	Algebra/Number Sense	134
Two-Dimensional Nim*	Logical Thinking/Spatial Reasoning	61
Value of Words*	Number Sense	33

* Indicates activities that can be used as openers with little or no adaptation.

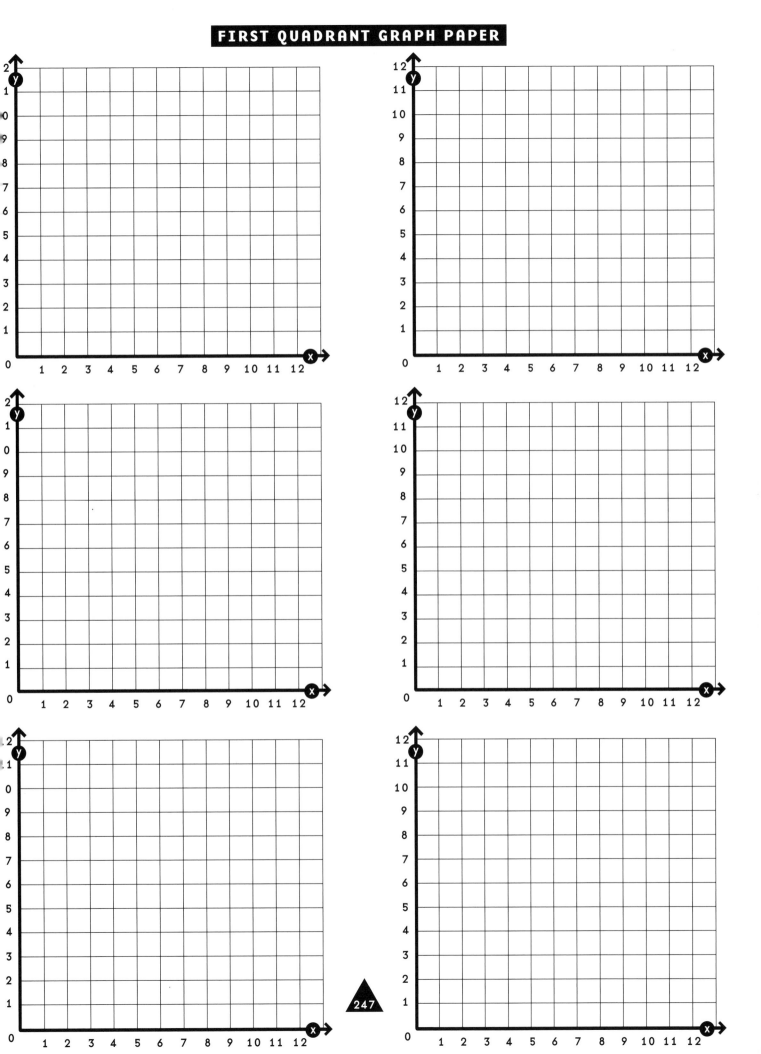

247

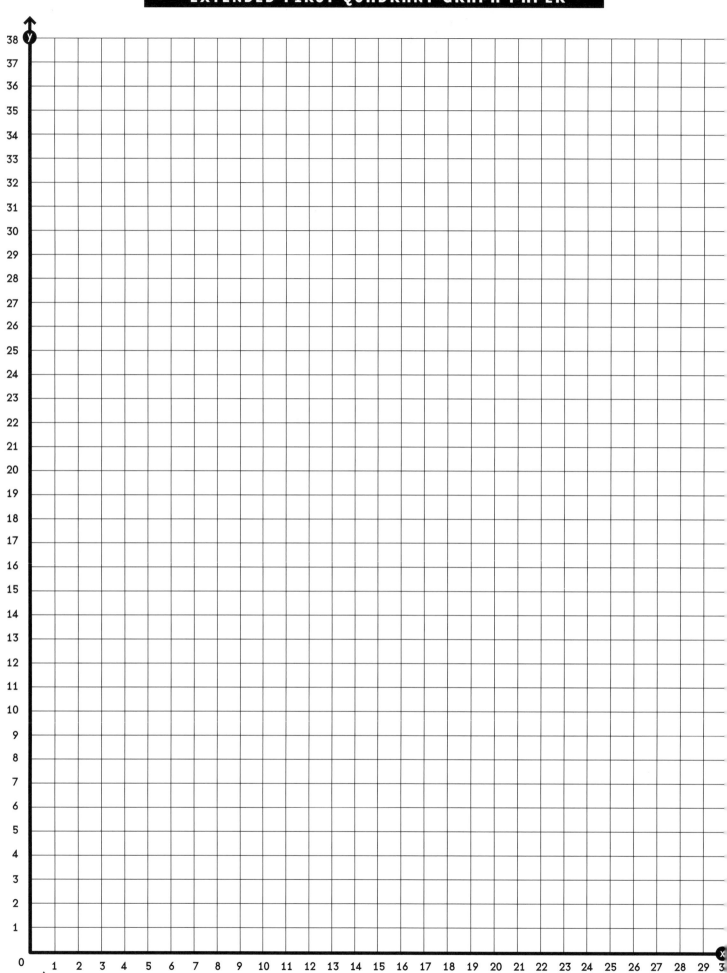

EQUALS: *FAMILY MATH–The Middle School Years*

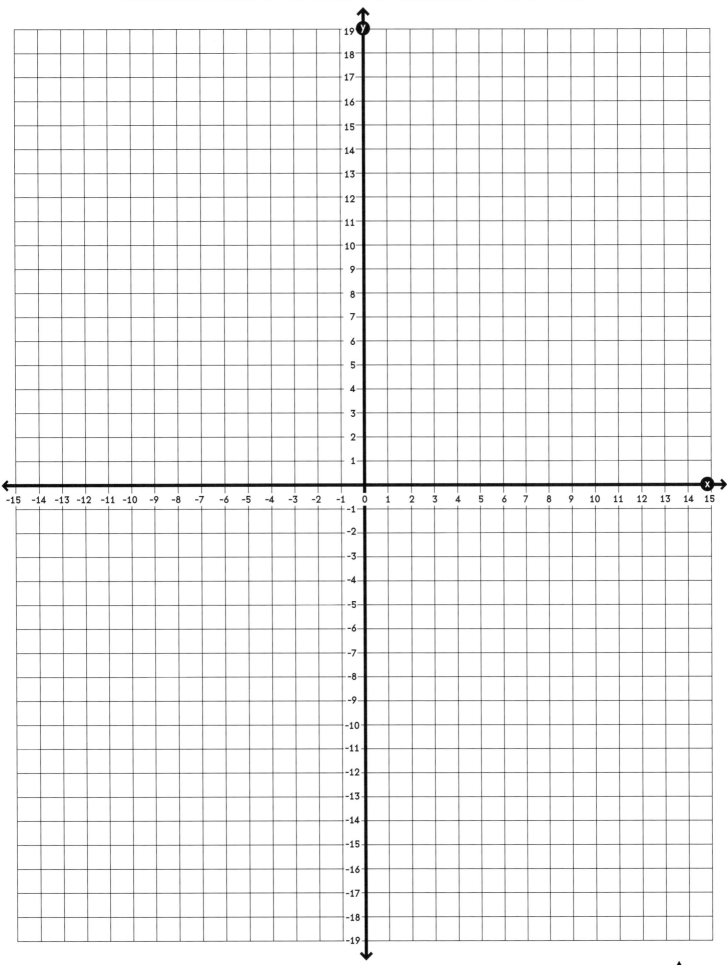

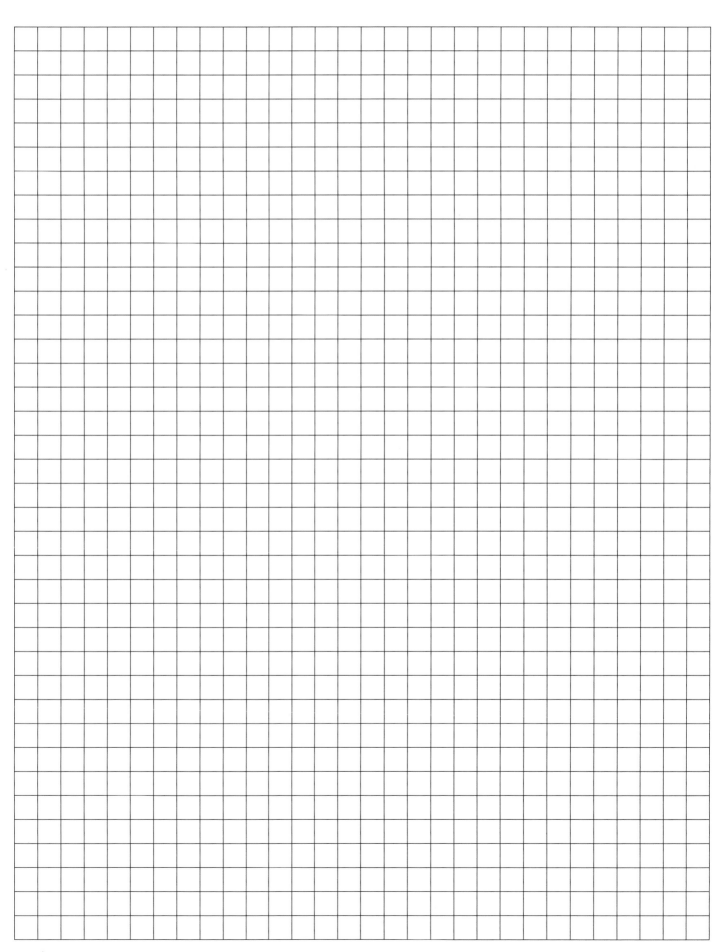

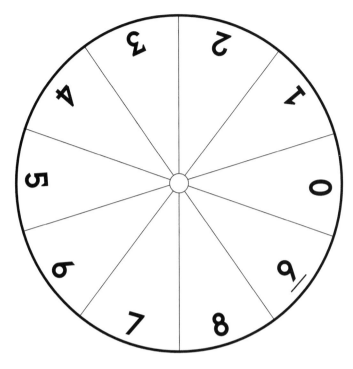

Hold a pencil point through a paper clip
at the center of the spinner and spin.

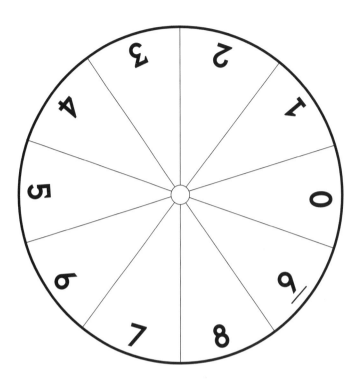

Hold a pencil point through a paper clip
at the center of the spinner and spin.

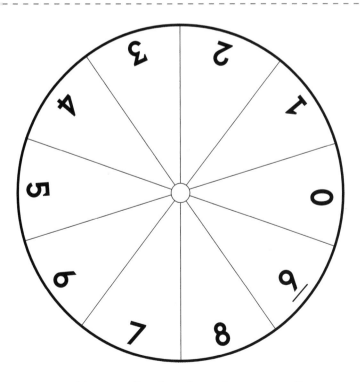

Hold a pencil point through a paper clip
at the center of the spinner and spin.

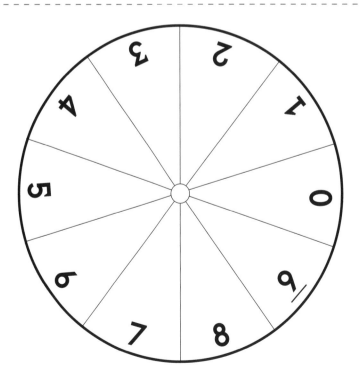

Hold a pencil point through a paper clip
at the center of the spinner and spin.

Hundreds Chart

1	2	3	4	5	6	7	8	9	10
11	12	13	14	15	16	17	18	19	20
21	22	23	24	25	26	27	28	29	30
31	32	33	34	35	36	37	38	39	40
41	42	43	44	45	46	47	48	49	50
51	52	53	54	55	56	57	58	59	60
61	62	63	64	65	66	67	68	69	70
71	72	73	74	75	76	77	78	79	80
81	82	83	84	85	86	87	88	89	90
91	92	93	94	95	96	97	98	99	100

Activity Types

The following icons indicate different types of activities. Some activities fit in more than one category.

 Openers: activities that work well as an opening station or whose first steps can be used as opening activities.

 Games: activities in a game format.

 Guided Activities: activities that require leader direction.

Algebraic Reasoning

Algebraic Estimation	Opener/Guided	
Area and Perimeter—Polyominoes	Guided	
Area and Perimeter—Rectangles	Guided	
Blocks and Beans: Visualizing Algebra Problems	Guided	
Buy One, Get One Free	Opener/Guided	
Cats and Canaries	Guided	
Flowerpots I	Guided	
Flowerpots II	Guided	
Four-Sock Drawers	Opener/Guided	
Getting to the Point	Guided	
Graphs to Equations	Guided	
Growing Cubes	Opener/Guided	
Growing Squares	Opener/Guided	
Half Empty, Half Full	Opener/Guided	
Hundreds Charts to Descartes I	Guided	
Hundreds Charts to Descartes II	Guided	
Math Behind the Trick I	Guided	
Math Behind the Trick II	Guided	
Patterns to Graphs	Guided	
Polyomino Puzzle Square	Guided	
The Doubling Problem	Opener/Guided	
The Guess and Check Method	Guided	
The Language of Algebra	Opener/Guided	
Twice as Big and More	Opener/Guided	
Zero Board Game	Game/Guided	
Zero Game	Game/Guided	
Zero Marker Games	Game/Guided	

Activity Types

Number Sense

Benchmarks: A Million Dollars and the Cost of Living	Guided	
Benchmarks: Apple and Microsoft	Opener/Guided	
Benchmarks: Time	Opener/Guided	
Calculating Patterns: Looking at Multiples	Opener/Guided	
Decimal Digit Cover Up	Game	
Decimal Double Digit	Game	
Digit Directives: Diminishing Division	Game	
Digit Directives: Finding Fractions	Game	
Digit Directives: Maximizing Multiplication	Game	
Exploring Divisibility Rules	Guided	
Exploring Number Sequences	Opener/Guided	
Fraction Calculator Explorations	Opener/Guided	
Fraction, Decimal, Percent Connection	Guided	
Mayan Mathematics	Game/Guided	
Nonconsecutive Number Boxes	Opener/Game	
Numerous Remainders	Opener/Guided	
Postage Problem	Guided	
Quick Calculations	Guided	
Resolving an Argument	Opener	
Resolving Another Argument	Opener	
Resolving a Third Argument	Opener	
Sharing the Whole	Opener/Guided	
Tax Collector Exploration	Game/Guided	
Ten, Twenty, Thirty	Game/Guided	
The Game of Euclid	Game/Guided	
The Game of Fifteen	Opener/Game	
Towers	Game	
Value of Words Revisited	Opener	

Tools for Parent Advocacy

College Catalog Information	Guided	
Uninformed Decisions	Guided	
Useful Math Survey	Guided	

These materials are appropriate for families with children in grades 5 to 8, unless otherwise indicated. Try your school and local libraries for copies of these resources.

101 Short Problems edited by Jean Kerr Stenmark. EQUALS, Lawrence Hall of Science, University of California at Berkeley, Berkeley, California, 1995.

A Mathematical Jamboree by Brian Bolt. A collection of interesting puzzles and activities, many of which can be adapted for families. Cambridge University Press, Cambridge, England, 1995.

Algebra in the Concrete by Mary Laycock and Reuben A. Schadler. Revised edition. Activity Resources Co., Hayward, California, 1987.

Algebra Puzzles and Problems by Carole Greenes and Carol Findell. Individual books for Grades 4, 5, 6, and 7. Creative Publications, Alsip, Illinois, 1998.

Beyond Facts & Flashcards: Exploring Math with Your Kids by Jan Mokros. Heinemann Publishers, Portsmouth, New Hampshire, 1996.

The Book of Think by Marilyn Burns. Little Brown & Co., Boston, 1976.

Creating Nim Games by Sherron Pfeiffer. Dale Seymour Publications, White Plains, New York, 1998.

Elementary School Mathematics: What Parents Should Know about Estimation by Barbara Reys. Hints and techniques for teaching estimation in real-life situations. National Council of Teachers of Mathematics, Reston, Virginia, 1982.

Elementary School Mathematics: What Parents Should Know about Problem Solving by Barbara Reys. Problem-solving techniques that connect to real-life experiences. National Council of Teachers of Mathematics, Reston, Virginia, 1982.

Estimation Explorations by Tom Murray. Grades 3–8. Activities that involve thinking, writing, and talking about estimation using whole numbers, geometry, measurement, fractions, and percents. Cusenaire Publications, White Plains, New York, 1997.

Exploring Everyday Day Math: Ideas for Students, Teachers, & Parents by Maya Apelman and Julie King. Grades K–6. Heinemann, Portsmouth, New Hampshire, 1993.

Exploring with Squares and Cubes by Ron Kremer. Cuisenaire Publications, White Plains, New York, 1997.

FAMILY MATH by Jean Kerr Stenmark, Virginia Thompson, and Ruth Cossey. Also available in Chinese, Spanish, and Swedish. EQUALS, Lawrence Hall of Science, University of California at Berkeley, Berkeley, California, 1986.

Helping Your Child Learn Math by Patsy Kantor. A collection of activities for everyday settings for children ages 5 through 13. Revised edition. U.S. Department of Education, Office of Educational Research and Improvement, Washington, D.C., 1998.

The I Hate Math Book by Marilyn Burns. Little, Brown & Co., Boston, 1975.

Key to... Workbook Sets: Key to Algebra, Key to Measurement, Key to Geometry, Key to Fractions, Key to Decimals, Key to Percents. Three to eight inexpensive books per set. Key Curriculum Press, Berkeley, California, 1992.

Maneuvers with Math Lab Books by D. Page, K. Chval, and P. Wagreich. The series includes *Maneuvers with Number Patterns, Circles, Fractions, Rectangles, Nickels and Numbers, Angles and Triangles*. Dale Seymour Publications, White Plains, New York, 1994.

Math Around the World by Beverly Braxton. GEMS, Lawrence Hall of Science, University of California at Berkeley, 1996.

Math at a Glance: A Month-by-Month Celebration of the Numbers around Us by Susan Ohanian. Heinemann, Portsmouth, New Hampshire, 1995.

Math Equals: Biographies of Women Mathematicians & Related Activities by Teri Perl. Grades 6 and up. Addison-Wesley, Menlo Park, California, 1978.

Math for Girls and Other Problem Solvers by Diane Downie, Twila Slesnick, and Jean Kerr Stenmark. EQUALS, Lawrence Hall of Science, University of California at Berkeley, 1981.

Math for Smarty Pants by Marilyn Burns. Little, Brown, & Co., Boston, 1982.

Math Power: How to Help Your Child Love Math, Even If You Don't by Patricia Kenschaft. Grades K–6. See especially, chapters 14 ("The Fifth Grade Crisis"), 16 ("How Drill and Kill Cripples U.S. Math Education"), and 17 ("Why Drill and Kill Holds U.S. Math Education Hostage"). Addison-Wesley, Menlo Park, California, 1998.

Number Sense: Simple Effective Number Sense Experiences by A. McIntosh, B. Reys, and R. Reys. Dale Seymour Publications, White Plains, New York, 1996.

Numbers: Facts, Figures and Fiction by Richard Phillips. A collection of facts about the numbers 1 through 156 and a few larger numbers. Cambridge University Press, Cambridge, England, 1994.

The Only Math Book You'll Ever Need by Stanley Kogelman and Barbara Heller. For adults. Dell, New York, 1988.

Puzzles, Mazes, and Numbers by Charles Snape and Heather Scott. A collection of interesting puzzles and activities, many of which can be adapted for family classes. Cambridge University Press, Cambridge, England, 1995.

*Using Calculators to Improve Your Child's Math Skill*s. National Council of Teachers of Mathematics (NCTM). Also available in Spanish. Free single copy available with stamped, self-addressed #10 envelope. (See in Publishers of Mathematics Education Materials section below for address.)

What Should I Look For in a Math Classroom? Annenberg/CPB Math and Science Project, P.O. Box 2345, S. Burlington, Vermont 05407-2345. Phone: 1-800-965-7373.

CD-ROM
Connecting the Past with the Future: Women in Mathematics and Science. Department of Mathematics, Western Illinois University, Macomb, Illinois, 1996.

Video
Mathematics: What Are You Teaching My Child? Featuring Marilyn Burns. Cuisenaire Publications, White Plains, New York, 1994. (20 minutes.)

Internet
America Goes Back to School <www.ed.gov/Family/agbts>

Connecting the Home, School, Community <www.sedl.org:80/hscp/welcome>

Family Educational Network <www.families.com>

Family Involvement Partnership for Learning <www.ed.gov/PFIE/index>

The Math Forum <http://forum.swarthmore.edu>

Parent Soup <www.parentsoup.com>

Urban/Minority Families <http://eric-web.tc.columbia.edu/families>

Magazines

Dynamath. Games and puzzles from all math topics. Some schools arrange to distribute this magazine in classrooms. Check with your child's teacher or order individual copies from the company. Scholastic Inc., P.O. Box 7503, Jefferson City, Missouri, 65102.

Games Junior. Ages 7 and up. P.O. Box 10147, Des Moines, Iowa, 50347.

Games Magazine. Middle school and up. P.O. Box 10147, Des Moines, Iowa, 50347.

Zillions. Children's version of *Consumer Reports.* Shows math surrounding purchasing decisions. Consumer Reports. P.O. Box 54861, Boulder, Colorado, 80322.

Publishers of Mathematics Education Materials

Activity Resources
20655 Hathaway Avenue
Hayward, CA, 94541
1-5l0-782-1300.

Creative Publications
5623 W. 115th Street
Alsip, IL 60803
1-800-624-0822.

Cuisenaire•Dale Seymour Publications
P. O. Box 5026
White Plains, NY 10602-5026
1-800-237-3142.

Heinemann,
361 Hanover Street
Portsmouth, NH 03801
1-800-793-2154.

Key Curriculum Press
P. O. Box 2304
Berkeley, CA 94702-9983
1-800-995-MATH.

National Action Council for
   Minority Engineering (NACME)
3 West 35th Street
New York, NY 10001-2281
1-212-279-2626

National Council of Teachers
   of Mathematics (NCTM)
1906 Association Drive
Reston, VA 20191-1593
1-800-235-7566.

Bibliography

Bibliography for FAMILY MATH Class Leaders and Teachers
Books, Pamphlets, and Reports

Addenda Series Grades 5-8: Developing Number Sense in the Middle Grades, Patterns and Functions, and Understanding Rational Numbers and Proportions. National Council of Teachers of Mathematics, Reston, Virginia, 1991.

Algebra by Anita Wah and Henri Picciotto. Creative Publications, Alsip, Illinois, 1994.

Curriculum and Evaluation Standards for School Mathematics. National Council of Teachers of Mathematics, Reston, Virginia, 1989.

Discovering Mathematics, The Art of Investigation by Anthony Gardiner. Clarendon Press, Oxford, England, 1987.

The Dream Keepers: Successful Teachers of African American Children by Gloria Ladson-Billings. Jossey-Bass, San Francisco, 1994.

Elementary Algebra by Harold R. Jacobs. W. H. Freeman and Co., San Francisco, 1979.

EQUALS Investigations: Telling Someone Where to Go, Scatter Matters, Growth Patterns, Remote Rulers, and Flea-Sized Surgeons. Five replacement units for the following topics: distance and angles, scatter plots and correlation, linear and exponential growth, reasoning and distance, and changes in scale. EQUALS, Lawrence Hall of Science, University of California at Berkeley, Berkeley, California, 1994.

Everybody Counts: A Report to the Nation on the Future of Mathematics Education, National Research Council, National Academy Press, Washington, D.C., 1989.

FAMILY MATH by Jean Kerr Stenmark, Virginia Thompson, and Ruth Cossey. Also available in Chinese, Spanish, and Swedish. EQUALS, Lawrence Hall of Science, University of California at Berkeley, Berkeley, California, 1986.

Figures, Facts, & Fables: Telling Tales in Science and Math by Barbara Lipke. Heinemann, Portsmouth, New Hampshire, 1996.

Getting Your Message Out to Parents by Nancy Litton. Math Solutions, Sausalito, California, 1998.

Bibliography

How Schools Shortchange Girls. American Association of University Women, Washington, D.C., 1992.

The Ideas of Algebra, K-12 (1988 Yearbook). National Council of Teachers of Mathematics, Reston, Virginia, 1988.

Innumeracy by John Allen Paulos. Hill and Wang Publisher, New York, 1988.

Let's Talk Math: Encouraging Children to Explore Ideas by Pat Lilburn and Pam Rawson. Heinemann, Portsmouth, New Hampshire, 1994.

"Making Inequality: Issues of Language and Meanings in Mathematics Teaching with Hispanic Students," by L. L. Khisty. *New Directions for Equity in Mathematics Education,* edited by W. Secada, E. Fennema, and L. Byrd. Cambridge University Press, Cambridge, England, 1995.

Math: Facing an American Phobia by Marilyn Burns. Math Solutions Publications, Sausalito, CA, 1998.

Mathematics: An Informal Approach by Albert B. Bennett, Jr. and Leonard T. Nelson. William. C. Brown Publishers, Dubuque, Iowa, 1988.

Mathematical FunFair by Brian Bolt. A collection of interesting puzzles and activities, many of which can be adapted for family classes. Cambridge University Press, Cambridge, England, 1989.

Multicultural and Gender Equity in the Mathematics Classroom: The Gift of Diversity (1997 Yearbook). National Council of Teachers of Mathematics, Reston, Virginia, 1997.

Multiplying Inequalities: The Effects of Race, Social Class and Tracking on Opportunities to Learn by Jeannie Oakes. RAND, Santa Monica, California, 1990.

A New Generation of Evidence: The Family is Critical to Student Achievement edited by Anne T. Henderson and Nancy Berla. The National Committee for Citizens in Education, Washington, D.C., 1994. Now distributed by Center for Law and Education, 1875 Connecticut Avenue, NW, Suite 510, Washington, D.C. 20009. 1-202-462-7688.

Number by John McLeish. Bloomsbury Publishing Limited, London, 1991.

"Race, Ethnicity, Social Class, Language and Achievement in Mathematics" by Walter G. Secada. In *Handbook of Research on Mathematics Teaching and Learning,* edited by Douglas A. Grouws, pp. 623-660. New York, Macmillan, 1992.

Reaching All Families: Creating Family-Friendly Schools edited by Oliver C. Moles. U.S. Department of Education, Office of Educational Research and Improvement, Washington, D.C., 1996.

"The Role of Parent Involvement in Children's Academic Achievement" by J. Bempecha. *School Community Journal.* Vol. 292, 1992. pp. 31-4.

Strong Families, Strong Schools, Building Community Partnerships for Learning. GOALS 2000, U.S. Department of Education, 600 Independence Avenue, SW, Washington, D.C. 20202, (800) USA-LEARN. Free brochure.

Introduction to TIMMS: The Third International Mathematics and Science Study, U.S. Department of Education, Office of Educational Research and Improvement, September 1997.

The World Book of Math Power, Vol. 1 and 2. World Book Encyclopedia, Inc., Chicago, 1983.

Index

Index

Notes